More Root Beer Advertising and Collectibles

Tom Morrison

4880 Lower Valley Road, Atglen, PA 19310

Acknowledgements

In addition to all those who contributed to the first book, I wish to thank the following for providing pictures, information and support in putting this second book together. Those who supplied pictures of their vast collections, I sincerely thank you: Jerome Gundrum, Jeff Bennett, Lyman Hensley, Ed Kochevar, Dave and Kathy Nader's *Root Beer Float* newsletter, Pettigrew Auction House in Colorado Springs, Bob Pirie, Dale Schatzberg, John Reece, Chris Weide, B.J. Cunningham, Charles Keck, Larry Bard, David Meinz, John Murphy, Jeni Olsze, John Quick, Hank Reidling, Reed Andrew, and Keith Austin.

A special thanks again to my lovely wife, Nancy, for her encouragement, sound advice, and understanding love.

Frostop display sign, approximately 10 feet high by 6 feet wide, found in Ashton, Idaho. *Picture courtesy of Reed Andrews.*

Book Layout by: Blair Loughrey

ISBN: 0-7643-0042-3
Printed in China
1 2 3 4

Published by Schiffer Publishing Ltd.
4880 Lower Valley Road
Atglen, PA 19310
Phone: (610) 593-1777; Fax: (610) 593-2002
E-mail: schifferbk@aol.com
Please write for a free catalog.
This book may be purchased from the publisher.
Please include $3.95 for shipping.
Try your bookstore first.

We are interested in hearing from authors with book ideas on related subjects.

Contents

Introduction

Welcome to the continuous world of root beer. Since my first book on root beer was published, another 338 brands have been discovered and substantiated. That brings the total to 1169 brands that we know so far, and there are still more!

After the first book, *Root Beer Advertising and Collectibles*, was published, it helped to open the field even more, especially for me. I met many nice people that I wouldn't have otherwise. Some were new collectors, some were advanced, some just had a question, some didn't know anything about root beer, some wanted to know how to start such a book, and some just wanted to exchange stories. I enjoyed them all, and have acquired many new found friends. That's what its all about!

Again, because of the first book, it was inevitable to do a second. There was just too much out there in root beer not to! This second edition was made possible by the grouping of some of the larger root beer collections in the nation. I thank those who took the time to take pictures and submit them.

As a result of some new items brought to light, it is possible that we collectors of root beer may have to change our way of thinking that Charles E. Hires was the first to invent root beer. More and more evidence, such as a few of the stoneware bottles, points to the fact that root beer existed *prior* to Charles E. Hires introducing his root beer extract to the public in 1876. In fact, some of the older bottles marked root beer are well before that date! The evidence is still inconclusive, but certainly makes for interesting discussion among collectors. All in all, it may turn out that root beer did exist in local pockets, but that Charles E. Hires was just the first to market it on a national basis.

With any collectible that becomes popular for a time, reproductions and fakes may appear quickly. Even root beer cannot escape. Fakes and reproductions have been identified here when known. Just be careful, as with anything, and know the item you are interested in.

If you are interested in furthering your knowledge or advancing your collection of root beer, my first book will give you more insight into root beer history, as well as valuable information about each category, i.e., cans, bottles, trade cards, mugs, bottle openers, etc. It is my hope that both books will give you some idea as to what may be available, and will help in enhancing your own collection. And remember......there's more out there!

Root Beer Regards,
Tom Morrison

A unique way of advertising your hobby!
(this is not the author's, but it's a great idea!)

More Little Known Tidbits

In the 1960s movie *The Parent Trap*, starring Haley Mills and Brian Keith (as her father), Brian Keith asks Haley Mills if she wants a root beer.

The 1967 movie *Hot Rods to Hell*, about thrill seeking juvenile delinquents and starring Dana Andrews, has a scene where a state police officer checks a girl's drink in a teenage hangout. As he smells it, she replies, "What's the matter, don't you know what root beer is?"

In the last scene of the 1991 movie *Fried Green Tomatoes*, starring Kathy Bates, the camera pans back to show old time signs, including some root beer ones, hanging on the front of the old cafe

In the 1995 movie *True Lies*, starring Arnold Schwarzenegger, a Dad's root beer sign is seen in the background as the actor walks through an antique store.

In the diner scene of the 1995 movie *The Bridges of Madison County*, starring Clint Eastwood and Meryl Streep, a root beer sign is displayed on the wall.

The song *Do You Remember,* by the Statler Brothers, mentions a double root beer float.

I Feel Lucky, a 1992 song by Mary Chapin-Carpenter, describes the singer going to a convenience store to buy a lottery ticket, where she also buys a pack of camels, a burrito, and a Barq's.

Root Beer Poem

Root beer, root beer, yes-sir-ee
That's the only drink for me;
Mighty tasty and healthy too,
It should be the drink for you.

Belly to the bar, brave and bold,
Ask for root beer, icy cold;
Enjoy the flavor, scream with delight,
Share with friends through the night.

Gulp it fast or sip it slow,
Either way, you'll like it so;
Buy it, try it, take some home,
Then come visit my "Hall of Foam."

—Tom Morrison
June 29, 1992

Root Beer Recipe

The following recipe for making your own root beer at home was found in a 1948 Stanwood Cookbook (Iowa):

1 to 3 cakes foam yeast
4 1/2 gallons fresh pure water (lukewarm)
2 quarts lukewarm water
4 lb. sugar
1 (3 oz.) bottle root beer extract

Soak yeast for 1/2 hour in 1 quart of lukewarm water. Place into a crock the sugar, root beer extract, and 4 1/2 gallons fresh pure water, slightly lukewarm. Strain soaked yeast through cheesecloth. Rinse yeast left on cloth with 1 quart of lukewarm water. Throw away solid particles. Add dissolved yeast and rinsing water to mixture in crock; mix well and bottle at once. Fasten corks securely. Keep in warm place for 3-6 days, depending on amount of yeast used. Cool and store in cold place.

Root Beer Clubs & Newsletters

Root Beer Float: a "focal point" newsletter for all categories of root beer memorabilia. This newsletter includes updates, questions, answers, articles, and classified ads for the root beer collector. Contact *Root Beer Float*, PO Box 571, Lake Geneva, WI 53147. The E-mail address is D.K.Nader@worldnet.att.net.

Root Beer Revelry: The official newsletter of The Society of Root Beer Cans and Bottles, this newsletter features nostalgic stories of root beer days gone by. The cost is $3 for six issues per year. Write to 1220 Cedar Avenue, Provo, UT 84604.

Soda-Net: This is the official newsletter of the Painted Soda Bottle Collectors Association (PSBCA), and is a great source for learning about and obtaining those root beer soda bottles. It features articles, pictures, history, reports, and trade/sell/buy ads. Membership is $17 for six issues per year. Contact PSBCA at 9418 Hilmer Drive, La Mesa, CA 91942, or via E-mail at aclsRus@msn.com.

Chapter 1
Bottles (ACLs)

More of these little bottle beauties have come forward. In total, there are 115 different brands of ACL (Applied Color Label) bottles that actually say "root beer" on the bottle. I am sure there are more waiting to be discovered, but that is the number known to exist at present.

In the first root beer book, the brand "B-K" was listed as an ACL bottle. That was in error and is not known to exist. In addition, the brand "Jud's" was misspelled as "Judd's."

Additional brands:

Brooks	Oke-E
Castle Rock	Old Dutch
Fisher's	Par-T-Pak
Glas Barrel	Raff's
Hill-Billy	Regent
Hi Port	Schroeder's
Hur-mon	Sugar Cane
Indian Club	Sunrise
Jic-Jac	Uncle Dan's
Kreemo	Vess
Lily Belle	Well's
Mother's Pride	Winner
N.B. Co.	Woosies

10-Erbs ACL bottle, 12 oz. $75-100.

Golden ACL bottle, by J.C. Gray, 12 oz., 3-color, c. 1991. $5-10.

Stratford "Johnny Bull" ACL bottle, 7 oz., c. 1959. $175-225.

Sugar Cane ACL bottles, 24 oz. each, c. 1940. Rare! Rare! $350-400 each.

Sunrise ACL bottle, 8 oz., clear glass (an amber exists). $150-200. The amber bottle would be $250-300.

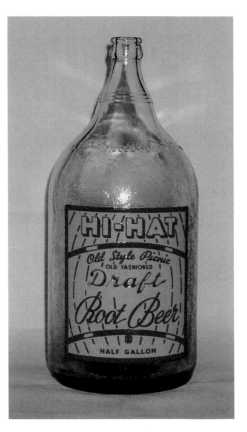

Hi-Hat ACL bottle, half gallon (64 oz.), c. 1945. $125-150.

Old Dutch ACL bottle, 10 oz., c. 1941 (most say beverages). $35-50.

Brooks ACL bottle, 28 oz. $100-125.

Hur-Mon ACL bottle, 32 oz. $100-125.

Mother's Pride ACL bottles. 10 oz., 1950.
64 oz., 1954. $150-200 each.

Castle Rock ACL bottle, amber glass, 12 oz.
Rare! $150-200.

Tom Sawyer ACL bottle, 30 oz. (8 and 12
oz. were featured in my first book, but the
quart is shown here because of its rarity).
$100-125.

Howel's ACL bottle, 64 oz. $50-75.

Hyde Park ACL bottle, 12 oz. $75-100.

Jud's ACL bottle, 12 oz., c. 1951. Embossed
name on shoulder. Rare! $350-400.

Papoose ACL bottle, 12 oz. $75-100.

Schroeder's ACL bottle, 12 oz., c. 1953. $150-175.

Mrs. Lombardi's ACL bottle, 12 oz., c. 1959. $100-150.

Papoose ACL bottle, 12 oz. (the 10 oz. is similar, but has an additional neck label). $100-125.

Quaker ACL bottle, 12 oz., clear glass, c. 1962. $25-35.

Quaker ACL bottle, 12 oz., amber glass, picture of barrel. $75-100. *Chris Weide collection.*

9

I.B.C. ACL bottle, 10 oz., c. 1964. $10-15.
Chris Weide collection.

Adams ACL bottle, 1/2 gallon, undated.
$100-125.

Missouri Club ACL bottle, 7 oz., 1946.
$100-125.

Oke-E ACL bottle, 7 oz., c. 1953. $150-175.
B.J. Cunningham collection.

Lily Belle ACL bottle, 8 oz., c. 1956. Rare!
Rare! Rare! Only one known in existence.
The broken top does not decrease the beauty
of this bottle. $175-200. *B.J. Cunningham
collection.*

Uncle Joe's ACL bottle, amber glass, 12 oz.
$25-35.

I.B.C. ACL bottles, 7 oz., 6 1/4" high. Name and brand are embossed, but the writing on reverse is ACL. Right: The "trial size" was distributed in 1992 with red & white lettering and is marked "this is a collector's limited edition bottle." Left: Distributed in 1993 with white lettering only, and is not marked "trial size." The "IBC story" on the reverse is not as long as the "trial size" version. $5-10 each.

Sonny O' Gold ACL bottle, 10 oz., amber glass, c. 1949. (this little beauty evidently was a "dug" bottle, as evidenced by the partial missing picture. At present, it is the only one known to exist). $175-200.

Mr. Root Beer ACL bottle, 10 oz., c. 1971. $30-40.

Frostie ACL bottle, 28 oz., c. 1949. Has "1-way beverage" on bottom and "Not to be Refilled" on shoulder. $30-40.

Uncle Dan's ACL bottle, 16 oz., 3-color, c. 1961. $50-60.

Wells ACL bottle, amber glass, 12 oz., 1952. $75-100.

11

Epping's ACL bottle, 12 oz. $75-100.

Green Spot ACL bottle, no ounce indicated, c. 1962. The reverse side is the same design but the letters are in Chinese! The bottom says "Los Angeles" so it is possible it was made for or in Chinatown. $150-200.

Cola "Indian Club" ACL bottle, 12 oz., 3-color. A similar bottle featured in my first book was also put out by the Cola Root Beer Co., but does not say "Indian Club" and is only one color (white). $100-125.

Kreemo ACL bottle, 12 oz., c. 1958. $75-100.

Vess ACL bottle, 16 oz., c. 1956. $35-50.

Uncle Tom's ACL bottle, 10 oz., c. 1953. A 32 oz. exists (this is a dual collectible in that when the bottle is filled, the contents darken the man's face, thereby featuring him as an African-American. This bottle is very difficult to find with "root beer" on it; most say "beverages"). $150-200.

Old Time ACL bottle, 12 oz., c. 1956. $35-50.

Zetz ACL bottles. Left: 12 oz., c. 1950. $35-50. Right: 12 oz., date unknown. $25-35.

Regent ACL bottle, 64 oz., c. 1951. $75-100.

N.B. Co., ACL bottle, amber glass, 10 oz. $150-200.

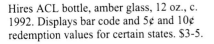

Carnation ACL bottle, 10 oz., amber glass, c. 1955. (does not have the picture of a carnation flower on the reverse, as the clear glass bottle in my first book does). $75-100.

Hires ACL bottle, amber glass, 12 oz., c. 1992. Displays bar code and 5¢ and 10¢ redemption values for certain states. $3-5.

Tower ACL bottle, amber glass, 28 oz., name embossed on neck, c. 1954 (the 7 oz. and 12 oz. are similar). $100-125.

Victory ACL Bottle, 10 oz., c. 1947. This is the hard to find two-color, more so than the one-color featured in my first book. $50-75.

YD ACL bottle, 28 oz., amber glass, name embossed on neck. $100-150. An identical 12 oz. exists.

Hi-Top ACL bottle, 7 oz., c. 1949. $25-35.

On-Tap ACL bottle, 10 oz., c. 1977. $15-25.

Honeymaid ACL bottle, 12 oz., c. 1939. $50-75.

Hill-Billy ACL bottle, 10 oz., c. 1952 (to many collectors, this one has the most detailed picture of all the root beers, and is a prize to own!). $150-200.

Rob's ACL bottle, amber glass, 10 oz., c. 1958. $75-100.

Woosies ACL bottle, 12 oz., name embossed on neck. Although it doesn't show "root beer" on the front, the reverse says "Only genuine Woosies root beer served in this bottle." $15-25. *Jerome Gundrum collection.*

Baker's ACL bottle, 1 pt. 12 oz., 3-color, 1940. $50-75. *Jerome Gundrum collection.*

Dad's stretch ACL bottle, 13". These stretch bottles are usually given away as prizes at carnivals and fairs. $5-10.

Smitty's ACL bottle, amber glass, 7 oz., label copyrighted 1949 (a 10 oz. also exists). $35-50.

Chapter 2
Bottles (Embossed)

Embossed bottles marked "root beer" are few and far between, and some are really works of art with intricate design. The embossing process is described in my first book. Extract bottles are not included here.

Additional brands:
- ABC
- Big Shot
- California
- Cronk, E.Y.
- Currier's
- Ford, Wm S.
- Nash, H.
- Neff, T.L.
- Owen's, C.B.
- Rathje & Hennessey
- Rathje & Maloney
- S.A. (San Antonio)
- South Bend
- Stites
- Torney, C.
- Yoman's

Rathje & Hennessey embossed bottle, quart, blob-top, c. 1890. $200-250.

Purdy's embossed bottle, 1 pt. & 10 fl. oz. $35-50. A similar 7 oz. also exists. *Dave & Kathy Nader collection.*

Portage embossed bottle, 7 1/2 oz., no date indicated. Says "Portage Root Beer Co., Portage, Wis." $25-35. *Dave & Kathy Nader collection.*

Hires embossed bottle, amber glass, no ounce indicated, date unknown. $15-20.

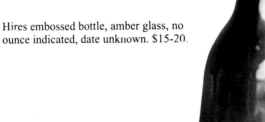

Big Shot embossed bottle, 12 oz., c. 1938. Embossed picture of a man with a cigar. $75-100.

E.Y. Cronk embossed bottle, green glass, blob-top, 7 1/4" high. $350-400. *Dave & Kathy Nader collection.*

S.A. embossed bottle, 10 oz. (San Antonio, Texas). $20-30.

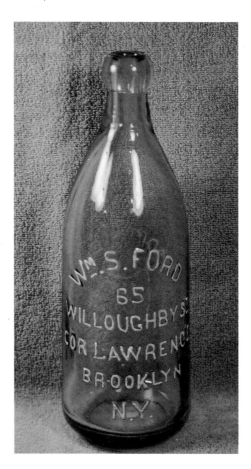

E.Y. Cronk embossed bottle, colbalt blue, blob-top, 7 1/4" high. $150-200. *Dave & Kathy Nader collection.*

H. Nash & Co. embossed bottle, colbalt blue, blob-top, 12-sided, 9 5/8" high, c. 1850-1860. Rare! $1200-1400. *Dave & Kathy Nader collection.*

Wm. S. Ford embossed bottle, blob-top, 10 1/2" high, says "Root Beer - 1878" on reverse. $100-150. *Dave & Kathy Nader collection.*

Stites embossed bottle, crown top, no ounce indicated. 8" high. $35-50. *Dave & Kathy Nader collection.*

S.H. Farnham embossed bottle, blob-top, 9 1/8" high. $75-100. *Dave & Kathy Nader collection.*

Currier's embossed bottle, Hutchison type, 6 3/4" high. $100-125. *Dave & Kathy Nader collection.*

California embossed bottle, blob-top, "Medicated." Has L&V trademark and 1876 date. 11" high. Dual collectible interest due to its year - a Centennial bottle. $375-500. *Dave & Kathy Nader collection.*

Lorenz embossed bottle, 1 pt. & 12 fl. oz., 11" high, c. 1940. $100-125. *Dave & Kathy Nader collection.*

C. Torney embossed bottle, blob-top, 10" high, says "C.T. Medicated root beer" on reverse. $100-125. *Dave & Kathy Nader collection.*

T.L. Neff's embossed bottle, blob-top, aqua glass, cork enclosure with lightning stopper, 10 1/4" high. "Pop & Premium." Has intertwining "TLN" trademark and "1876" on reverse. Dual interest collectible as a Centennial bottle due to the year. $250-300. *Dave & Kathy Nader collection.*

Rathje & Maloney embossed bottle, 11" tall, letters "R&M" intertwined on front. Reverse says "Rathje & Maloney, 578 Fourth Ave, Brooklyn, New York" trademark, 1890. $100-125. *Jerome Gundrum collection.*

Royal Crown bottle, embossed on both sides. See detailed information about Royal Crown in my first book. This bottle is marked "Mancuso Bros. Morgan City, Louisiana," and has the markings of "3R*" (which is the mark of the Three Rivers Glass Co., Three Rivers, Texas). $150-200. *Ramiro Davila collection.*

T.L. Neff's embossed bottle, blob-top, 11" high. Has trademark and "1889" on reverse. $150-200. *Dave & Kathy Nader collection.* 19

Chapter 3
Bottles (Paper Label)

Paper labels do not have a long life span! Try washing the bottle and see what happens to the paper label. It was a cheaper process than the ACLs; labels were slapped on a clean bottle and then out the door they went. Paper labels were more detailed with beautiful artwork, and could be mass produced to accommodate needed quantity.

Additional brands:

Allouez	East Side	Kist	Pilzenbaur
American	Eclipse	Klich's	Pioneer Valley
American Home	Elk's	Kool Club	Rawhide Red
American Sports	Falcon	Kroger's	Rock Creek
Arizona	Filbert	Lasser's	Rocky River
Arctic	Frank's	London Dry	Roscoe's
B-Lion Club	Gary's	Magoo's	Roxo
Barrel Of	Glickco	Manhattan	Royal Flush
Baumeister	Greene, J.L.	McCarter's	S&S
Bell Hop	Gruber	Mega	Sanitary
Belton's	Harkavy	Meyers	Silver Cup
Big Five	Hekelnkaemper	Miller-Becker's	Silver Spring
Bison Brew	Bros.	Montreal	Snapple
Bonnie Miss	Henry	Mystic Seaport	Sunshine
Brillion	Henry Weinhard	National	Superfine
Broadcast	Hopper's Dining	Naturale 90	Swallo
Cadillac	Car	Nehi	Tastee Club
Classic Selection	Hrobak's	Nottingham	Thomas Kemper
Colfax	Hydrox	Old Abe	Tom Mix
Cray's	Iron Horse	Old Colony	Twin-Kiss
Doc's	Jack Sprat	Old Scotch	Victoria Pier
Dog 'n Suds	Jax	Osceola-Spruce	Virginia Dare
Dr. Tima	Kazmaier	Peacock	Waterhouse
	Killebrew	Penn	Winchester

Arizona paper label, 19 oz., "Root beer float - real ice cream soda taste." This was a 1995 trial test for different flavors in several national sites. $3-5.

Silver Cup paper label, 1/2 gallon. Phone number is Armitage 1216 - Chicago. $25-35. *Charles Keck collection.*

Rawhide Red paper label, 12 oz., c. 1995. $5-10.

Paper labels. Left: Virginia Dare, 1 qt.
Right: Bonnie Miss, 32 oz. $15-20 each.
Dale Schatzberg collection.

Bruce's paper label, 1 qt. $5-10. *Larry Bard
collection.*

Paper labels. Left: Klich's, 1 qt. Right:
Kroger's Latonia Club, 24 oz. $15-20 each.
Dale Schatzberg collection.

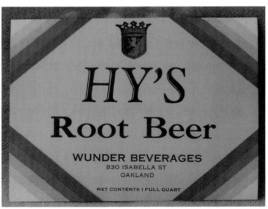

Hy's paper label, 32 oz., 3 1/4" x 4 1/2". $3-
5.

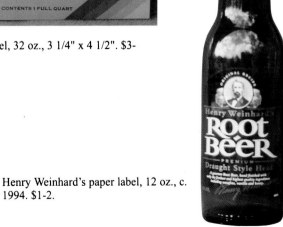

Henry Weinhard's paper label, 12 oz., c.
1994. $1-2.

Eli Lilly paper label on 1 gallon amber jug,
extract flavoring. $15-20. *Dale Schatzberg
collection.*

21

Classic Selection "The Gulpster," 1 liter, paper label, plastic bottle. First found at the 7-11 convenience store in 1995. $1-2.

Quaker paper label, 1/2 gallon. $30-40. *David Meinz collection.*

Polar paper label, 1 liter plastic bottle. $1-2.

Virgil's paper label, 15.2 oz., amber bottle, porcelain stopper with wire bale type top. Imported from England by Crowley Beverage Co. of Wayland, Massachusetts, and recently available in the United States, c. 1993. $3-5.

Colfax paper label, 7 oz. $10-15. *Dale Schatzberg collection.*

Winchester paper label, 22 oz., c. 1994. $5-10.

Paper labels, recent vintage, 12 oz.: L-R: Victoria Pier (restaurant) from Alton, New Hampshire; Magoo's (drive-in restaurant) from Goffstown, New Hampshire; Gary's (Gary's drive-in) from Keene, New Hampshire; Bison Brew (Dakota restaurant) in Avon, Connecticut, c. 1994; J.L. Greene's from Columbus, Ohio. $3-5 each. *Jerome Gundrum collection.*

Lost Trail paper label, 12 oz., currently on market on limited distribution. $5-10 for 6-pak.

Belfast Mug paper label, 11 oz., c. 1950. $25-30 for 6-pak.

Barq's paper label, "Soviet Union out-of-business sale," a special limited promotion (expired September 30, 1992) to acquire "Soviet stuff" (such as medals, ribbons, patches, emblems, etc) by sending in a proof of purchase label and 50 cents for one item of non-choice. $5-10 for 12-pak; $3-5 for liter.

Dr. Tima paper label, 10 oz., c. 1979. $3-5.

J.C. Gray's paper label, plastic bottle, 1 1/2 liters, c. 1990. $3-5.

Mega paper label, 2 liters, plastic bottle, c. 1992. $1-2.

Jack Sprat paper label, 24 oz. $5-10.

Hires paper label, 12 oz., picture of "Diplomas and medals awarded," c. 1890. $15-20.

Paper labels. L-R: Silver Spring, 10 oz., c. 1978; Naturale 90, 10 oz., c. 1990; Osceola, 10 oz., c. 1974 (crown shows a yellow and black smiley face). $2-5 each.

Krueger paper label, 12 oz., label dated 1937. $5-10.

Thomas Kemper paper label, 12 oz., bar code is on side. Currently being brewed as of 1996. $1-3.

Gruber paper label, 30 oz., c. 1965. Bottle is embossed on neck and heel with "Gruber" name. $10-15.

"Barrel Of" paper label, 64 oz., c. 1982, amber glass. Bottle is barrel shaped/ designed. $15-20.

Broadcast paper label, 24 oz. $5-10.

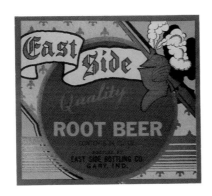

East Side paper label, 24 oz. $5-10.

American paper label, 7 oz. $5-10.

Paper labels: Left: American Sports Bar All Stars, 12 oz., c. 1991. Right: Roscoe's, 10 oz., reverse has picture of a drive-in restaurant. $3-5 each.

Hekelnkaemper Bros. paper label. Indications are it may be for a gallon syrup jug. $3-5.

25

Bellhop paper label, 32 oz. $10-15.

Bobby's paper label, 1/2 gallon. $5-10.

Hopper's Dining Car root beer paper label, 12 oz. $5-10.

Paper labels: Left: Baumeister, 12 oz., c. 1940. $5-10. Right: Snapple, 16 oz., c. 1992. $1-3.

Paper labels: Left: Iron Horse, 12 oz., c. 1990. Right: Killebrew, 12 oz., c. 1992, "Features Minnesota grown honey." And yes, this is Harmon Killebrew, the famous baseball player! $3-5 each.

American Home paper label, no ounce indicated, but probably 1 qt. (neck label missing). $5-10.

Royal Flush paper label, 1 qt., c. 1947. $25-30.

B-Lion Club paper label, 1 pt. 8 oz. $15-20. *Dave & Kathy Nader collection.*

Pilzenbaur paper label (neck label indicates brand). $10-15. *Dave & Kathy Nader collection.*

Swallo paper label, 12 oz., green glass. $10-15. *Dave & Kathy Nader collection.*

Big Five paper label, no ounce indicated. $10-15. *Dave & Kathy Nader collection.*

Rocky River paper label, 1 pt. 8 oz. $10-15. *Dave & Kathy Nader collection.*

Filbert paper label, 1 qt., green glass. $10-15. *Dave & Kathy Nader collection.*

Superfine paper label, 1 pt. 8 oz. $10-15.
Dave & Kathy Nader collection.

S&S paper label, 24 oz. $10-15. *Dave &
Kathy Nader collection.*

Peerless paper label, 24 oz. $10-15. *Dave &
Kathy Nader collection.*

Sanitary paper label, 1 pt. 8 oz. $10-15.
Dave & Kathy Nader collection.

Old Abe paper label, 32 oz. $15-20. *Dave &
Kathy Nader collection.*

Hydrox paper label, 32 oz. $10-15. *Dave & Kathy Nader collection.*

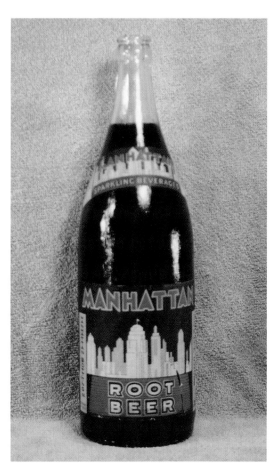

Manhattan paper label, 32 oz. $15-20. *Dave & Kathy Nader collection.*

Peacock paper label, 32 oz. $15-20. *Dave & Kathy Nader collection.*

Ma's paper label, 32 oz. $10-15. *Dave & Kathy Nader collection.*

Brillion paper label, 32 oz. $10-15. *Dave & Kathy Nader collection.*

Blatz paper label, 1 pt. 8 oz. $15-20. *Dave & Kathy Nader collection.*

Old Colony paper label, 32 oz. $10-15. *Dave & Kathy Nader collection.*

Montreal paper label, 32 oz., green glass. $15-20. *Dave & Kathy Nader collection.*

Hires paper label, 32 oz., green glass, foil-covered top. $15-20. *Dave & Kathy Nader collection.*

Henry's syrup jug paper label, 1 gallon. $5-10. *Dale Schatzberg collection.*

Belton's syrup jug paper label, 1 gallon. $5-10. *Dale Schatzberg collection.*

Nehi syrup jug paper label, 1 gallon. $5-10. *Dale Schatzberg collection.*

Snyder's flavored syrup paper label, 1 pt. $15-25. *Dale Schatzberg collection.*

L-R: Dog 'n Suds paper label qt. bottle; 16 oz. aluminum can; 4-pak of 12 oz., c. 1995. $2-3 each. *Dale Schatzberg collection.*

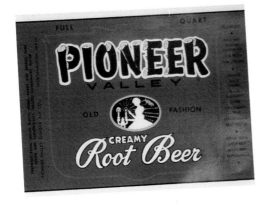

Paper labels: Pioneer Valley, 1 qt., from Northampton, Massachusetts; Purity, 1 pt. 14 oz., from Wilmington, Delaware. $3-5 each. *Jerome Gundrum collection.*

Tastee Club paper label, 12 oz., from Wilmington, Delaware. $3-5. *Jerome Gundrum collection.*

Rock Creek paper label, 1 pt. 8 oz., from Washington DC. $3-5. *Jerome Gundrum collection.*

Penn paper label for flavored syrup, gallon size. $5-10. *Jerome Gundrum collection.*

Paper labels: Simpson Spring, 28 oz., from South Easton, Massachusetts; Swallow's, 12 oz., from Lima, Ohio. $3-5 each. *Jerome Gundrum collection.*

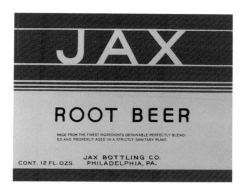

Waterhouse paper label, 12 oz., from Windham, New Hampshire. $1-2. *Jerome Gundrum collection.*

Jax paper label, 12 oz., 3" x 4", from Philadelphia, Pennsylvania. $3-5. *Jerome Gundrum collection.*

Paper labels: McCarter's, 12 oz., from Philadelphia, Pennsylvania; Meyer's "Fizz," 32 oz., from Bethlehem, Pennsylvania. $3-5 each. *Jerome Gundrum collection.*

Paper labels: Old Fashion, 12 oz., dated 1939, from Erie, Pennsylvania; Old Scotch, 12 oz., from Philadelphia, Pennsylvania. $3-5 each. *Jerome Gundrum collection.*

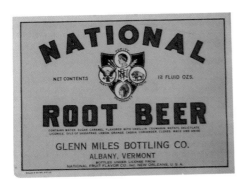

National paper label, 12 oz., from Albany, Vermont. $3-5. *Jerome Gundrum collection.*

Manhattan paper label, 3" x 7", offers the bottle with this label for 5¢. $3-5. *Jerome Gundrum collection.*

Paper labels: Lasser's, no ounce indicated, from Chicago, Illinois; London Dry, 7 oz., from Wilmington, Delaware. $3-5 each. *Jerome Gundrum collection.*

33

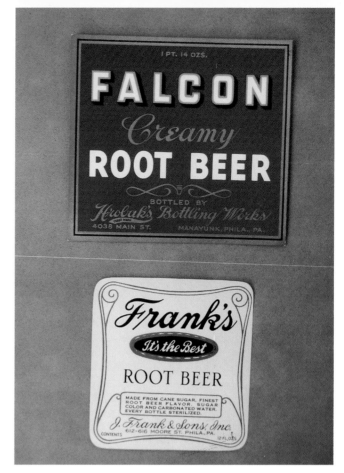

Paper labels: Kist, no ounce indicated, from Rockport, Massachusetts; Kool Club, 12 oz., c. 1938, from Wilmington, Delaware. $3-5 each. *Jerome Gundrum collection.*

Paper labels:. Falcon, 1 pt. 14 oz., from Philadelphia, Pennsylvania; Franks, 12 oz., from Philadelphia, Pennsylvania. $3-5 each. *Jerome Gundrum collection.*

Cray's paper label, 32 oz., 4 1/8" x 4 3/8", from Holyoke, Massachusetts. (Note: this is the same company as P.J. Cray's, which has the pottery bottle featured in my first book). $3-5. *Jerome Gundrum collection.*

Arctic paper label, no ounce indicated, 4 3/4" x 3 1/2", from Philadelphia, Pennsylvania. $3-5. *Jerome Gundrum collection.*

Doc's paper label, 12 oz., c. 1947, from New York, New York. $3-5. *Jerome Gundrum collection.*

Howel's paper labels. Top is 1 pt. 8 oz.; bottom is 32 oz. $3-5 each. *Jerome Gundrum collection.*

Paper labels. From top: Harkavy, from New York; Hrobak's, 12 oz., from Manayunk, Pennsylvania; Hy's, 12 oz., from Oakland, California. $3-5 each. *Jerome Gundrum collection.*

Twin-Kiss paper label, 1/2 gallon syrup bottle. $12-15. *Jerome Gundrum collection.*

Eclipse syrup bottle, paper label, 1 pt. $8-12. *Jerome Gundrum collection.*

Chapter 4
Bottles (Stoneware)

Stoneware root beer bottles have been around for a long, long time. In fact, it is these particular bottles that lead us to question whether Charles E. Hires was the first to discover root beer in 1876, as some of these bottles are much older than that. This evidence leads root beer collectors to think that perhaps Charles E. Hires was just the first to distribute his popular root beer on a national basis. While this evidence isn't totally conclusive and has not yet been accepted as fact (at least by this collector), it does present possibilities to ponder.

In my first book, the brand "Krass" was misspelled. It should have been "Kraas".

Additional brands:

Avery Lord	Evans & Barney	Mansfield, P.
Beckemeier, Wm.	Gaylor, J.	McEvoy, J.
Becude, A.G.	Gleason, F.	McLean's, S&J
Boston	Harris, J.W.	Milliman's, J.
Burr & Waters	Hogan, M.	Nay's
Callaghan, A.	L&W	Robinson's
Chester, J.	Lake & Ewing	S&S White
C.P.	Lake, J.	Toby's
Dillion, P.	Lamb, J.	Waddington, H.
Dr. Smith	Leonard, A.	Well's
Eddy, A.	Luce, D.	Woodward
	Manns, F.	Woolsey's

Vreeland's Indian stoneware bottle, 10" high. $125-175. *Dave & Kathy Nader collection.*

Boyd & Beard stoneware bottle, says "root beer" on reverse side. 10" high. $175-200. *Dave & Kathy Nader collection.*

J. Chester stoneware bottle, says "root beer" on reverse side. 9 3/4" high. $100-125. *Dave & Kathy Nader collection.*

M. Hogan stoneware bottle, says "root beer" on reverse side. 9 1/2" high. $100-125. *Dave & Kathy Nader collection.*

J. Lamb stoneware bottle, says "root beer" on reverse side. 9 5/8" high. $100-125. *Dave & Kathy Nader collection.*

Wm. Kraas celebrated root beer stoneware bottle, 9 3/4" high, 12-panel sided, date unknown. $100-125.

J. Mcevoy stoneware bottle, says "root beer" on reverse side. 9 1/4" high. $125-150. *Dave & Kathy Nader collection.*

Ledger's stoneware bottle, 8 oz., 7" high. $75-100. *Jerome Gundrum collection.*

Fargo stoneware bottle, two-tone, crown top, 7 5/8" high. $100-125. *Dave & Kathy Nader collection.*

Wagner Bros. stoneware bottle, 7 1/2" high. $100-125. *Dave & Kathy Nader collection.*

Robinson stoneware bottle, 9 1/8" high. $125-150. *Dave & Kathy Nader collection.*

De Freest stoneware bottle, 9 1/2" high. $100-125. *Dave & Kathy Nader collection.*

Tobey's Knickerbocker stoneware bottle, 9 1/2" high. $125-150. *Dave & Kathy Nader collection.*

Woolsey's stoneware bottle, 8 1/2" high. $150-175. *Dave & Kathy Nader collection.*

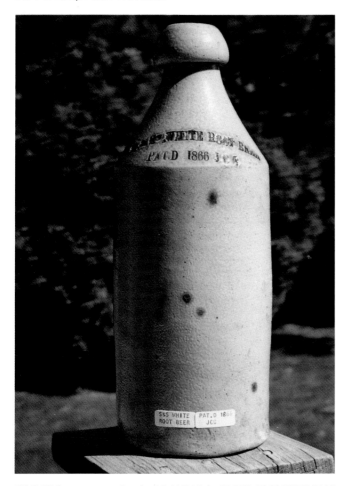

S&S White stoneware bottle, 10 1/4" high, "PATD 1866 JCS." $100-125. *Dave & Kathy Nader collection.*

Avery Lord stoneware bottle, 9 1/2" high. $100-125. *Dave & Kathy Nader collection.*

Woodward stoneware bottle, 10 3/4" high. $100-125. *Dave & Kathy Nader collection.*

Burr & Waters stoneware bottle, 9 5/8" high. $100-125. *Dave & Kathy Nader collection.*

Nay's stoneware bottle, 10" high. $100-125. *Dave & Kathy Nader collection.*

Nay's stoneware bottle, 10" high. $100-125. *Dave & Kathy Nader collection.*

Chapter 5
Cans

More aluminum, pull-tabs, steel, pop-tops, rolls, large seams, small seams. Cans! Cans! Cans! Combined with the 388 cans featured in my first book, the total of different brands is nearing the 500 mark. Once those still undiscovered are added, I am sure the number will be well over 500!

Additional brands:

Albertson's A+
American Super
Autocrat
Bashas
Big Chief
Big Star
Bireley's
Blue Ridge
Bohack
Bond Street
Byrne
Cal Fresh
Carousel
Cayna
Colleigiate
Comic Can
Copa
Costa
Cost Cutter
Cushman's
Daper Dan
Davy Crockett
De Moulas
DF
Di-Ett
Dominicks

Domonts
Eagle
E-Z Diet
Farm House
Fastco
Fed Cal
Fiesta
Filberts
Filigree
Flair
Food Fair
Food Giant
Fred's
Freshie
Furrs
Giant
Glee
Glueck
Grand Taste
Greatland
Green Rivers
Heritage
High Rock
Holipop
Homeland
Jobi
Julep

Kewpie
King Kullen
King Soopers
Kwik Trip
Land O'Lakes
Liday
M
Made Rite
Manhattan
Mat
MDI
Mississippi
Mountain Stream
Mr. Fizz
My-T-Fine
Old Keg
Pik-A-Pop
Plenty Good
Pop
Presidents Choice
Push
Randall's
Real Value
Re-Joyce
Rich Life
Roy Rogers
Rush

Sam's Choice
Schwegmann
Seaway
Select
Sensational
Shop 'n Save
Silver Cup
Snapple
Society Club
Soda Barrel
Speedee
Suncrest
Sunny Select
Tease
Thinny-Thin
Tomboy
Top Pop
Treasury
Vermont Pop
Victory
White Swan
Wilson Farms
Winbrook
Zip

Cans: Left: Wawa, 12 oz. $10-15. Right: Stop-N-Go, 12 oz. $3-5.

Dad's cone-top can, 12 oz. $20-30.

Cans: Old Dutch, 16 oz.; Alaska, 12 oz. $10-15 each.

Fastco (Fareway Stores); Sam's Choice (Walmart), c. 1992; Select (Safeway Stores), c. 1993. $1-2 each.

Cans: L-R: Chug A-Lug, Weis, Meijer. All 12 oz. $5-10 each.

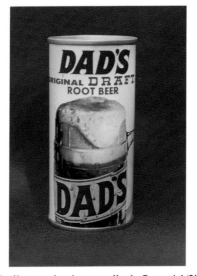

Dad's can, aluminum, pull tab, 7 oz., 4 1/2" high. An unusual size! $5-10. *John Reece collection.*

Albertson's A+ can, 12 oz., c. 1995. $1-2.

C&C Super can, 9 oz., cone top, c. 1950s. $10-15.

Old Keg cans, 12 oz., aluminum. $1-2.

Cans: Holipop, American Super, Richfood, Domont's, Julep. All 12 oz. $5-10 each.

Cans: L-R: Sunny Select, Kwik trip, Greatland. All 12 oz. $1-2 each.

Randall's aluminum can, 12 oz. Distributed by Randall's Food Markets Inc., Houston, Texas. $1-2.

Marquee can, aluminum, 12 oz., c. 1993. $1-2.

Bala Club cone-top can, 12 oz., c. 1950s. $35-45.

President's Choice can, 12 oz., aluminum, c. 1992; Ralph's Private Selection can, 12 oz., aluminum, c. 1993. $1-2 each.

Chapter 6
Dispensers

Dispensers come in all sizes, shapes, and compositions. They include porcelain, china, stainless steel, wood/crockery, plastic, glass, and so on. And surprisingly, they are not all root beer! In fact, root beers comprise only a small percentage of dispensers. There are more root beer dispensers than featured here; unfortunately, the pictures were not available. Further information on dispensers may be found in my first book.

Additional brands:
Dr. Swett's
Liberty
Vigorex

Rochester barrel dispenser, wooden, counter top size, 19 1/2" high, 12" diameter, 3 steel side emblems, manufactured by J. Hungerford Smith. $800-1200. *John Reece collection.*

Liberty barrel dispenser, wooden, inside crock-lined, 14 1/2" high, 8" diameter; crock liner is 7 1/2" deep. Manufactured by Multiplex Faucet Co., St. Louis, Missouri. $800-1200. *Courtesy of John Murphy, Morral, Ohio.*

Generic brand barrel dispenser, metal, 24" high, 20" diameter. $75-100. *Dale Schatzberg collection.*

Buckeye syrup dispenser. No information available. $250-300. *Courtesy of Jeni Oleze.*

Buckeye Barrel dispenser, wooden, counter top size, 13" high, 9" diameter, manufactured by Multiplex Faucet Co., St. Louis, Missouri. $300-400. *Dave & Kathy Nader collection.*

Buckeye syrup dispenser, porcelain, 15" high, distributed by Cleveland Fruit Juice Co., Cleveland, Ohio., dated August 17, 1915. $1200 (auction, 1994). *Courtesy of Pettigrew Auction House, Colorado Springs, Colorado.*

Dr. Swett's syrup dispenser, porcelain, bottle shaped. No other information available. $700-800.

Magnus syrup dispenser, porcelain, 13 3/4" high, has the word "ATCO" on bottom. $600 (auction, 1994). *Courtesy of Pettigrew Auction House, Colorado Springs, Colorado.*

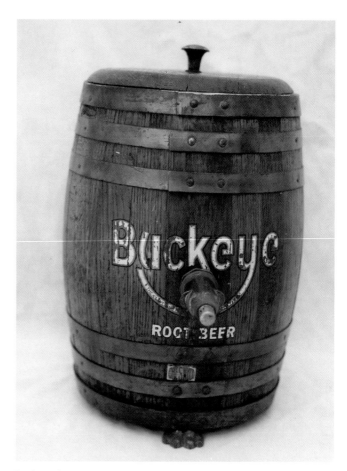

Alber's syrup dispenser, porcelain, push-button spout, 10 1/2" high. $350-400. *Jerome Gundrum collection.*

Buckeye barrel dispenser, wooden, counter top size, brass bands, crock-lined inside, 13 3/4" x 8". Manufactured by Cleveland Fruit Juice Co., Cleveland, Ohio. $300-400. *Jerome Gundrum collection.*

Bowey's syrup dispenser, porcelain, 15" high. $1300 (auction, 1994). *Courtesy of Pettigrew Auction House, Colorado Springs, Colorado.*

Dr. Swett's barrel dispenser, wood and brass, copper lined, name on both sides, 23 1/4" high, 12 1/4" diameter at top. Right spigot marked "Pat July 30, 1901." $300-400. *Jerome Gundrum collection.*

Middleby syrup dispenser, amber glass, push button spout, 12" high, 7" diameter. $500-700. *Hank Reidling collection.*

Rochester syrup dispenser, ceramic, 12 1/2" high, spigot marked "Pat'd Sept 4, 1917 C&H NY." $375-400. *Jerome Gundrum collection.*

Murray's syrup dispenser, ceramic, 12 1/2" high. Nearly the same as the Rochester (probably made by the same company, but not marked). Unfortunately, this one was made into a lamp! $375-450 as original. *Jerome Gundrum collection.*

Buckeye syrup dispenser, porcelain, 13 1/2" high, pump type. "Cleveland Fruit Juice Co., Cleveland, Ohio" stamped in base; "11-7-1919" on bottom. $400-450. *Jerome Gundrum collection.*

Hires syrup dispenser, porcelain, 11 1/4" high without pump, 7 3/4" diameter at bottom. $400-500. *Jerome Gundrum collection.*

Chapter 7
Mugs (ACLs)

Root beer mugs have become very popular to collect. Whether for root beer only or as part of a larger mug collection, each mug has its own story and history. In more cases than not, root beer mugs epitomize a small drive-in somewhere, sometime, and each conjures up a cherished memory. A "root beer toast" to those special drive-in hamburger places!

Additional Brands:

Big Rooty	Mug
Birchwood	Mug-Belfast
Hersey	Rowland's
Maid Rite	Skeet
Miklo	Sno-cap

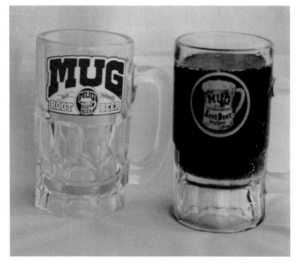

Left: Mug ACL mug, 3-color, 6". $10-15.
Right: Older Belfast Mug logo, 6". $15-20.

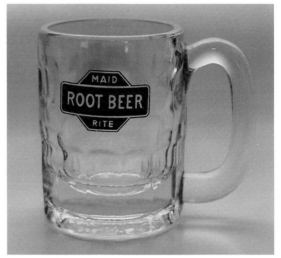

Maid Rite ACL mug, 4 1/2". $10-15. *Dale Schatzberg collection.*

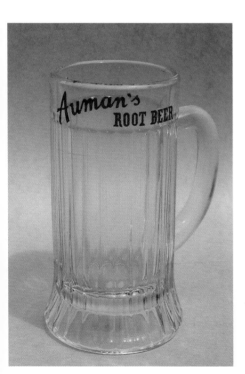

Auman's mug, ACL, 7", flaired bottom. $20-30. *Dale Schatzberg collection.*

Birchwood ACL mug, 5 1/2". $10-15. *Dale Schatzberg collection.*

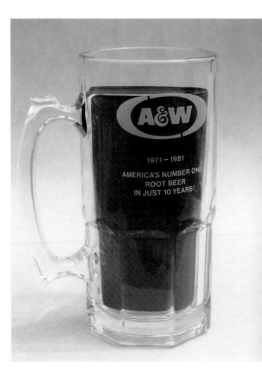

A&W mug, 6", etched. "1971-1981 America's number one root beer in just 10 years." $10-15. *Dale Schatzberg collection.*

Stewart's mason-style
jar, no handle, 5". $2-5.

Frostie ACL mug, 4 1/2". $10-15.

Hires ACL mug, 4 1/2", c. 1980's. $5-10.

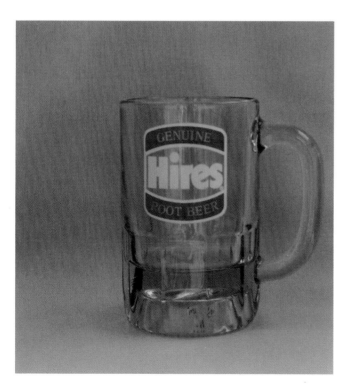

Hires ACL mug, 5". $5-10.

Skeet ACL mug, 4 1/2". $20-25. *Dale
Schatzberg collection.*

1919 mason-style mug, ACL, double-sided logo, 5 1/8" high, c. 1993. $3-5.

Stewart's ACL mug, vertical panels, 5 7/8" high, c. 1920s. $15-25.

Richardson ACL mug, 5 3/8" high. Normally in red, the white is extremely difficult to find. $15-20.

A&W ACL mug, 5 3/4", promoting the company's 75th anniversary in 1994. A 7" mug also exists (8 colors? Some say 7, some say 6!). $5-10.

Sno-cap mug, ACL glass, 4 1/2". $20-25. *Jerome Gundrum collection.*

Chapter 8
Mugs (Pottery)

The words "pottery" and "stoneware" are normally used in place of each other, even though there really is a difference. For our purposes here, they are both considered the same.

Many of these mugs are very, very rare, but that does not take away the opportunity of admiring them.

Additional brands:

Bardwell's	Murray's
Barnet's	Nesden
Canadian Club	Paramount
Connor's Amberglo	Pixie
C.P.	Red Diamond
Fox	S&H
MacKinnon's	Standard
Meco	Weidman

Miner's mug, pottery. Flip side features a miner swinging a pick. Reference this as Type 1. $250-300.

Miner's mug, pottery, 4 3/4" high. Reference this as Type 2. $200-225. *Dave & Kathy Nader collection.*

Gold-Bond mug, pottery, 4 1/2" high. Manufactured by Denison Bottling Co. $80-105. *Jerome Gundrum collection.*

Hires mug, pottery, 5" high. "Made in Germany for the Charles E. Hires Co., Villeroy & Boch, 'Mettlach' #2327." $150-200.

Bowey's mug, pottery, picture of a bowey sea marker, 4 1/2" high. $100-150. *Dave & Kathy Nader collection.*

C.P. mug, pottery, 3 7/8" high. $30-40.

Red Diamond mug, pottery, 6 1/4", "The Liquid" Carbonic Company. $150-200. *Dave & Kathy Nader collection.*

Hunter's mug, pottery, 6 3/8". $75-100. *Dave & Kathy Nader collection.*

Armour's "Veribest" mug, pottery, 6" high (most likely from the "Armour's Meat Co."). $50-75.

Canadian Club pottery mug, 5" high, handle at rear. Only one known in any collection. $200-250. *Dave & Kathy Nader collection.*

MacKinnon's mug, pottery, 4 3/4" high. $125-150. *Jerome Gundrum collection.*

Richardson's Liberty mug, pottery, 5 1/16" high. $80-105. *Jerome Gundrum collection.*

Bardwell's mug, pottery, 4 7/16" high, made by White's Pottery in Utica, New York. $150-175. *Jerome Gundrum collection.*

Chapter 9
Signs & Emblems

Here are a lot more signs! A special thank you to Jerome Gundrum for making his vast sign collection available. This rare opportunity to view many signs that most of us will never see elsewhere, is very much appreciated.

Kemp's sign, tin, 14" x 19 3/4", very early sign. "Crown, Cork & Seal Co., Baltimore, USA." $150-175. *Jerome Gundrum collection.*

Rochester sign, tin, 20" x 30". $85-110. *Jerome Gundrum collection.*

Reed & Bell sign, porcelain over tin, 27 3/4" x 35 1/2". $225-275. *Jerome Gundrum collection.*

Virginia Dare sign, tin, embossed, 13 3/4" x 19 5/8", "Burdith Co., NY." $90-110. *Jerome Gundrum collection.*

Howel's sign, tin, 10 3/4" x 23 1/2", "Robertson-Dualife - Springfield, Ohio." $75-100. *Jerome Gundrum collection.*

Rochester sign, tin, 17" x 23 1/2". $65-85. *Jerome Gundrum collection.*

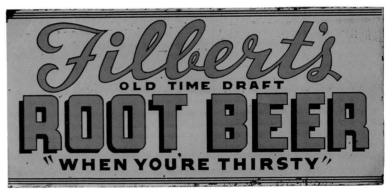

Filbert's sign, tin, 10" x 22". $65-85. *Jerome Gundrum collection.*

Ted's sign, tin, 6 1/4" x 11". Desperate Sign Co., Wadsworth, Ohio. Note: this sign is a fake. Not known to exist originally, it was copied from the cardboard bottle carrier, which has the same lettering style and wood grain, but shows a mug of root beer rather than Ted swinging a bat. $8-12. *Jerome Gundrum collection.*

Stewart's sign, tin, self-framed. "Stout Industries Inc., St Louis, Mo. Cable Car Beverage Corp, Denver, CO. 1990." $20-35. *Jerome Gundrum collection.*

Ted's sign, tin, embossed, 10" x 15". Desperate Sign Co., Wadsworth, Ohio. This sign is also a fake. No original tin sign like this is known to exist. This one was copied from a 1950's poster for Ted's root beer. Note: this sign does display the original bottle, not the fake bottle. $8-12. *Jerome Gundrum collection.*

Kist sign, tin, embossed, self-framed, 19 1/2" x 27". "Drink." Stout Sign Co., St Louis, Missouri. $85-110. *Jerome Gundrum collection.*

Allen's sign, tin, embossed, 11" x 14". This is a new, fake sign, made recently by enlarging an original Allen's root beer extract trade card. A sticker on the plastic the card was wrapped in said "made in China." $5-10. *Jerome Gundrum collection.*

56

Kist sign, tin, embossed, self-framed, 12 3/4" x 19 1/2". "Big Bottle." $85-110. *Jerome Gundrum collection.*

Howel's sign, tin, 19 3/8" x 27 1/4". $75-100. *Jerome Gundrum collection.*

Howel's signs. A comparison of the 11 3/4" x 16 5/8" reproduction sign (small one) to the original. The reproduction is self-framed and is made by the AAA Sign Co., Coitsville, Ohio. $8-12. *Jerome Gundrum collection.*

Rob's sign, tin, embossed, self-framed, 11 1/2" x 29 1/2". $85-110. *Jerome Gundrum collection.*

Detail of the top of the Howel's bottle-shaped, di-cut signs. The reproduction on the right is identified by the indention of the sign's outer edge near the bottle cap.

Howel's sign, tin, bottle-shaped di-cut. Left: Original, 29 1/2" x 8 5/16". $200-250. Right: Reproduction, 29 5/8" x 8 1/2". $100-150. AAA Sign Co., Coitsville, Ohio. Note: both signs say "Robertson-Dualife - Springfield, Ohio". See the close-up pictures for details of the difference. *Jerome Gundrum collection.*

Close-up of the Howel's bottle-shaped, di-cut signs, showing details of the difference. The reproduction on the right has a black cuff and vertical lines in the elf's face.

Belfast thermometer, tin, 8" x 27 1/2", c. 1950. $120-145. *Jerome Gundrum collection.*

Krueger sign, tin, embossed, self-framed, 9 1/2" x 27 1/2". Stout Sign Co., St Louis, Missouri. $100-125. *Jerome Gundrum collection.*

Gran'pa Graf's sign, tin, embossed, 9 3/4" x 27 1/2". Scioto Sign Co., Kenton, Ohio. $85-100. *Jerome Gundrum collection.*

Gran'pa Graf's sign, tin, embossed, self-framed, 12" x 27 1/2". Stout Sign Co., St. Louis, Missouri. $100-125. *Jerome Gundrum collection.*

Old Fashion sign, tin, 19 1/2" x 29 1/2". $85-105. *Jerome Gundrum collection.*

Sprecher sign, tin, embossed, self-framed, 12" x 20", c. 1985. $35-50. *Jerome Gundrum collection.*

Buckeye sign, aluminum, 7" x 12". $35-50. *Jerome Gundrum collection.*

Buckeye sign, tin, 18" x 24", "Cleveland Fruit & Flavor Co." $85-110. *Jerome Gundrum collection.*

Buckeye sign, tin, di-cut, self-framed, 17 3/4" x 23". $100-120. *Jerome Gundrum collection.*

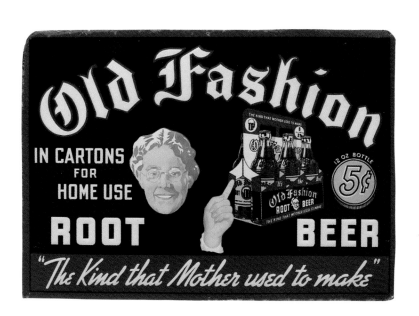

Old Fashion sign, tin, embossed, 19 1/2" x 28", Novelty Art Co., Coshocton, Ohio. $135-160. *Jerome Gundrum collection.*

Lyon's sign, tin, bottle-shaped, di-cut, 12" x 45", "No. 305 Stout Sign Co., St Louis, MO." $150-175. *Jerome Gundrum collection.*

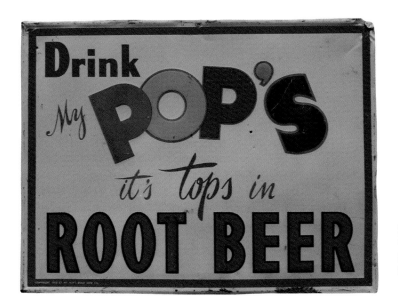

My Pop's sign, tin, embossed, 17 3/4" x 24", "Copyright 1948 by My Pop's Root Beer Co. advertiser's service." $100-125. *Jerome Gundrum collection.*

Nesbitt's sign, tin, embossed, 9" x 17 1/2". $50-75. A twice-as-large identical sign exists. *Jerome Gundrum collection.*

No brand name sign, reverse painting on glass, 6" x 15". This was part of a 1940s Coca-Cola display. $50-75. *Jerome Gundrum collection.*

High rock sign, tin, embossed, 8" x 20". Novelty Advertising Co., Coshocton, Ohio. $65-85. *Jerome Gundrum collection.*

Old Dutch sign, tin, embossed, self-framed, 17 1/2" x 35 1/4". $100-125. *Jerome Gundrum collection.*

Kay-C sign, tin, embossed, 12" x 24". $75-100. *Jerome Gundrum collection.*

Old Dutch thermometer, tin, 13 1/2" x 5 3/4". $65-85. *Jerome Gundrum collection.*

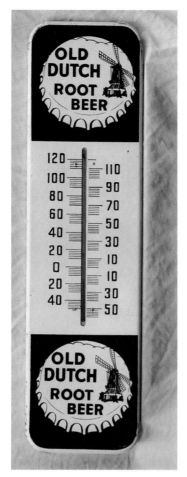

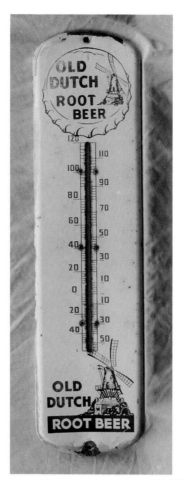

Old Dutch thermometer, tin, 7" x 26 1/2". $100-125. *Jerome Gundrum* collection.

Old Dutch thermometer, tin, 7" x 26 1/2". $100-125. *Jerome Gundrum collection.*

Kay-C sign, tin, embossed, 12" x 24", J.V. Reed & Co., Louisville, Kentucky. $75-100. *Jerome Gundrum Collection.*

Uncle Smilie's sign, tin, approx 13" x 30", 7-Up bottling Co., Duluth, Minnesota. $100-150. *Jon Quick collection.*

63

Mason's thermometer, tin, embossed, 9 3/4"
x 25 5/8". $75-95. *Jerome Gundrum
collection.*

Old Dutch sign, tin chalkboard, 18" x 35". $100-125. *Dave & Kathy
Nader collection.*

Frostie sign, tin, embossed, 12 1/2"
diameter. A similar 38" sign exists. Stout
Sign Co., St Louis, Missouri. $65-85.
Jerome Gundrum collection.

Mason's thermometer, tin, 4 1/2" x 15". $45-
60. *Dave & Kathy Nader collection.*

Hires sign, tin, 12" diameter. $50-75. An identical 24" sign exists. *Dave & Kathy Nader collection.*

Cloverdale sign, tin, embossed, self-framed, 17 1/2" x 24". Novelty Advertising Co., Coshocton, Ohio. $100-125. *Dave & Kathy Nader collection.*

Palmer's barrel sign, curved porcelain, dimensions unknown. $400-600. *Courtesy of Jerome Gundrum.*

Auman's sign, reverse painting on glass, 12" x 16". $200-250. *Dale Schatzberg collection.*

Yankee Doodle sign, tin, embossed, self-framed, 12" x 18". $150-200. This is a "real dandy" sign!

Hires sign, cardboard, di-cut, 11 1/4" x 13 3/4", c. 1900. Baby's left leg is hinged to allow backward movement for a 3-point stance so as to appear to be crawling. Head is slotted at neck for back and forth movement. $700-800.

Thomas Kemper paper poster, 18" x 24", 1994. $15-20.

Hartshorn's advertisement for its extract, possibly a poster, cut and mounted on press board, 10 1/4" x 14 1/2". $15-20.

Dr. Swett's sign, cardboard, 10" x 17", c. 1950s. $50-75.

Hires paper poster, 10" x 14", 1976, Hickory Inc., Carson City, Nevada (an identical 14" x 20" sign exists, dated 1981). $5-10.

Frostie thermometer, tin, 8" x 36 1/2". $50-75.

Fanta wall mount light, plastic, electric, ll" x 8" x 4". $25-35. *Dale Schatzberg collection.*

Hires lighted sign, electric, plastic front. 6 1/4" x 15 1/4", c. 1950s. $20-30.

Magnus emblem, heavy gauge metal, 5 3/4" x 12". $85-100. *Jerome Gundrum collection.*

Lash's curved barrel emblem, porcelain over tin, 6 5/8" x 15 3/4". $175-225. *Jerome Gundrum collection.*

Rochester curved barrel emblem, aluminum, 7 3/4" x 11 1/2". $35-50. *Jerome Gundrum collection.*

Hunter's dispenser emblem, tin, embossed,
4 1/4" x 7 1/2". $35-50. *Jerome Gundrum
collection.*

Crescent license plate attachment, tin, 4" x
11", covered with tiny glass beads for
reflecting light at night. $35-50. *Jerome
Gundrum collection.*

Smith-Junior curved barrel emblem, tin, 9" x
15". $100-125. *Jerome Gundrum collection.*

Bowey's curved barrel emblem, di-cut, mug
shaped, 7" x 10". $65-85. *Jerome Gundrum
collection.*

Richardson's barrel emblem, heavy cast
metal, 9" x 16". $75-100. *Dale Schatzberg
collection.*

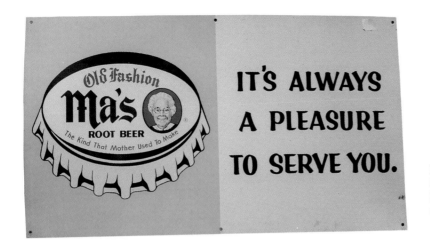

Ma's sign, tin, 13 1/2" x 24", "Permanent Sign & Display Co., Inc., Reading, Pennsylvania." $50-75. *Dale Schatzberg collection.*

Howel's sign, tin, 24" diameter, American Art Works Inc., Coshocton, Ohio, #M-160. $85-100. *Dave & Kathy Nader collection.*

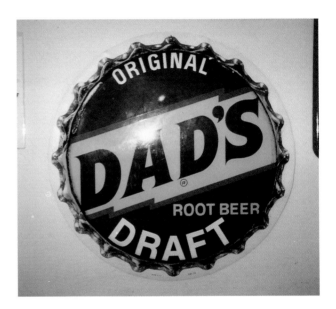

Dad's sign, tin, 30" diameter, bottle cap shaped, manufacturer unknown but marked #PM-10. $85-100. *Dave & Kathy Nader collection.*

Mason's sign, tin, bottle cap shaped, 41" x 50 1/2". Stout Sign Co., St Louis, Missouri, #M-4256. $65-85. *Dave & Kathy Nader collection.*

Twang sign, tin, 11 3/4" x 27 3/4". $65-85.
Dave & Kathy Nader collection.

B-K sign, porcelain over heavy steel, 30" x
45". $150-200. *Dave & Kathy Nader
collection.*

Hires "Josh Slinger" sign, lithograph, 6 1/2"
x 10". Copyright 1914 by the Charles E.
Hires Co., Philadelphia, Pennsylvania.
$300-500. *Dave & Kathy Nader collection.*

Hires sign, tin, self-framed, embossed, 19 7/
8" x 25 3/4", "Printed in USA, No. 419.
Hires is a registered trademark of Beverages
International Inc., Evanston, IL." $45-65.
Jerome Gundrum collection.

Belfast Mug thermometer, tin over cardboard, 8 7/8" diameter, "Permanent Sign & Display Co., Inc., Reading, PA" on reverse. $75-95. *Jerome Gundrum collection.*

Hires sign, cardboard, di-cut, 11 3/8" x 9 13/16", lower right marked "Litho in USA, M-2." $65-85. *Jerome Gundrum collection.*

Pennsylvania Dutch sign, celluloid over cardboard and tin, 9 1/8" x 14 9/16". "100-L.B. Copyright 1955 JU-C-Orange of American" marked in lower left corner. $125-150. *Jerome Gundrum collection.*

Stewart's sign, porcelain, 9" x 12", new.
$12-15. *Jerome Gundrum collection.*

Hires sign, cardboard, easelback, 17 15/16"
x 11 15/16", marked "Litho in USA, Form
No. B1-3." $55-75. *Jerome Gundrum
collection.*

Rochester sign, paper, 11 3/4" x 8 15/16".
$25-40. *Jerome Gundrum collection.*

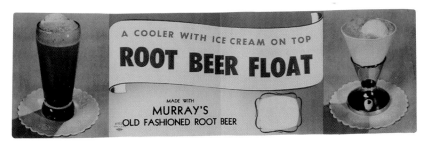

Murray's sign, paper, 6" x 20". $8-12.
Jerome Gundrum collection.

Rader's sign, tin, embossed, 13 3/4" x 19 5/8". "The Donaldson Art Sign Co., Cov. KY." $250-300. *Jerome Gundrum collection.*

Dad's poster, paper, 13 15/16" x 11 1/16", advertising the Dad's "Helio-Jet" toy. More information on this toy can be found in my first book. $12-18. *Jerome Gundrum collection.*

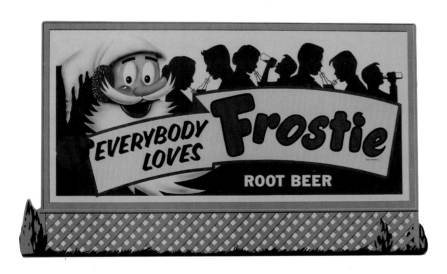

Frostie sign, cardboard, di-cut, easelback, 12 9/16" x 22 11/16" (note that sign is designed like a roadside billboard!). $50-65. *Jerome Gundrum collection.*

Richardson's sign, tin, self-framed, embossed, 18" x 36". $125-150. *Jerome Gundrum collection.*

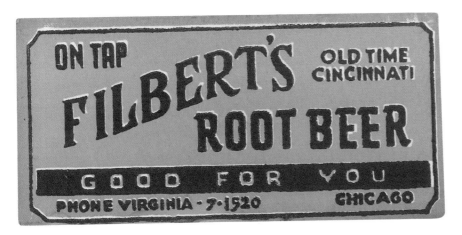

Filbert's sign, cardboard, 5" x 10 1/2". $15-25. *Jerome Gundrum collection.*

Triple XXX sign, di-cut tin, embossed, 10" x 25 5/8". Marked "M2-50" at bottom (notice the bullet holes!!). $150-175. *Jerome Gundrum collection.*

Dad's sign, tin, 10" x 28 1/2", features the "Papa" 1/2 gallon size. $75-100. *Jerome Gundrum collection.*

Ma's sign, tin, 5 9/16" x 17 5/8", Scioto Sign, Kenton, Ohio. $50-75. *Jerome Gundrum collection.*

Ma's sign, cardboard, easelback, 23 13/16" x 35 3/4", "Litho in USA" (Note: the "7" is pasted over some other number below the "5¢"). $45-65. *Jerome Gundrum collection.*

Mason's sign, tin, l9 1/4" x 27". $55-85.
Jerome Gundrum collection.

Dr. Swett's sign, enamel over tin, 35 1/2" x
59 5/8", marked "S-47-209." $350-400.
Jerome Gundrum collection.

Richardson's sign, plaster, 3-dimensional, 7
15/16" x 6 1/2". $40-65. *Jerome Gundrum
collection.*

Ma's sign, tin, 13 1/2" x l9 1/2", embossed.
$75-100. *Jerome Gundrum collection.*

Mason's sign, tin, self-framed, embossed,
12" x 30", Stout Sign Co., St Louis, MO,
"M-110." $100-125. *Jerome Gundrum
collection.*

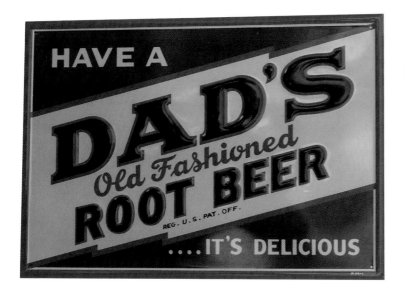

Dad's sign, tin, embossed, 18 7/8" x 26 7/8",
marked "PM-1". $85-105. *Jerome Gundrum
collection.*

Dad's tin signs: Top: 11" x 14", marked "S-
1." $50-75. Bottom: 22 1/8" x 30 3/16",
marked "S-4." $85-110. *Jerome Gundrum
collection.*

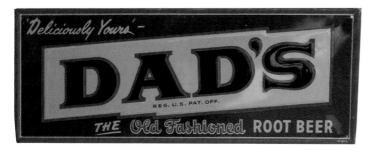

Dad's signs, tin, self-framed, embossed,
both 11 3/4" x 30 7/8" and marked "PM-2."
$85-105 each. *Jerome Gundrum collection.*

A&W sign, tin, 35 1/2" diameter, early logo.
$135-175. *Jerome Gundrum collection.*

Richardson sign, enamel over tin, embossed, 8 9/16" x 23 5/8". $125-150. *Jerome Gundrum collection.*

Richardson sign, tin, 26 3/8" x 29". "Robertson - Springfield, Ohio" (a much larger, identical sign is pictured in my first book). $125-150. *Jerome Gundrum collection.*

Barq's sign, enamel over tin, double-sided (wall bracket not seen), 19 7/8" x 27 7/8", marked "Donasco 4-47." $175-200. *Jerome Gundrum collection.*

Richardson sign, tin, embossed, self-framed, 18" x 36". $125-150. *Jerome Gundrum collection.*

Frostie sign, "Cameo bottle," plastic over metal, 4 1/4" x 9 3/8", marked "6-53." $35-50. *Jerome Gundrum collection.*

Frostie sign, tin, self-framed, 9 7/8" x 27 15/16", marked "Press Sign Co - St Louis 12-64, Printed in USA, SO-16." $75-100. *Jerome Gundrum collection.*

Mason's thermometer, tin, 25 9/16" x 9 3/4". $100-125. *Jerome Gundrum collection.*

Dad's thermometer, tin, embossed, 25 5/8" x 9 13/16". $100-125. *Jerome Gundrum collection.*

Hires thermometers, tin, bottle shaped, di-cut, all 7 5/8" x 28 5/8". Marked on bottom from L-R: "BN-16," "BN-16," and "4145." $95-125 each. *Jerome Gundrum collection.*

Frostie's thermometers, tin, 11 5/8" x 3 1/16", middle and right are marked "SO-17, made in USA." $45-65 each. *Jerome Gundrum collection.*

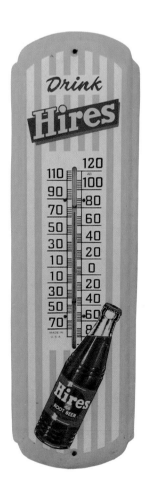

Hires thermometer, tin, 8" x 27". $75-100. *Jerome Gundrum collection.*

Triple XXX thermometer, tin, 7" x 27". $100-125. *Jerome Gundrum collection.*

Dr. Swett's thermometer, tin, 5" x 17". $75-85. *Jerome Gundrum collection.*

Dad's thermometers, tin, both 27 1/8" x 7 1/4", and marked "PM-TH-1." Right only: Press Sign Co., St Louis 63107. $75-100 each. *Jerome Gundrum collection.*

Hires "Josh Slinger" sign, tin, 9 1/8" x 16 1/4", "copyright 1914 Charles E. Hires Co., Philadelphia, PA" (Note: about 1"-1 1/2" has been cut off of left side). $250-300. *Jerome Gundrum collection.*

Hires sign, tin, "Flapper Lady", embossed, 13 3/4" x 19 5/8", "Made in USA, B-l-(9)." $250-300. *Jerome Gundrum collection.*

Hires sign, paper, 7" x 27", c. 1920s. $150-175. *Jerome Gundrum collection.*

Hires sign, "Red Hat Lady", tin, 9 3/4" x 27 5/8", embossed, marked "Made in USA, B-8." $250-300. *Jerome Gundrum collection.*

Hires sign, tin, embossed, 3 1/4" x 9 1/4". $35-55. *Jerome Gundrum collection.*

Hires sign, tin, embossed, 7 3/4" x 35 7/8", "Chas. W. Shonk Co., Litho. Chicago No. E4024." $135-165. *Jerome Gundrum collection.*

Hires sign, porcelain over tin, 12" x 30", "Ingram - Richardson, Beaver Falls, Pennsylvania; 100 Williams St., NY." $200-250. *Jerome Gundrum collection.*

Hires sign, tin, embossed, 9 3/4" x 27 3/4", marked "B-37." $135-165. *Jerome Gundrum collection.*

Hires sign, tin, embossed, 9 7/8" x 27 5/8". $125-150. *Jerome Gundrum collection.*

Hires sign, tin, embossed, 9 7/8" x 27 1/2". $115-135. *Jerome Gundrum collection.*

Hires sign, tin over cardboard, 5 15/16" x 8 7/16", marked "FA-2." Donaldson Art Sign Co., Covington, Kentucky. $45-65. *Jerome Gundrum collection.*

Hires sign, porcelain over tin, ll" x 28", "Made in USA Code GBB." $250-300. *Jerome Gundrum collection.*

Hires sign, tin, embossed, 9 5/8" x 13 5/8", "Made in USA, BT-2." $65-85. *Jerome Gundrum collection.*

Hires sign, thin tin, embossed, 9 5/8" x 27 5/8", "Made in USA, BM-1." $50-75. *Jerome Gundrum collection.*

Hires sign, tin, 7" x 12". $35-55. *Jerome Gundrum collection.*

Hires sign, tin, embossed, 12" diameter, "CA-1." $50-75. *Jerome Gundrum collection.*

Hires sign, tin, self-framed, embossed, 13 3/8" x 39 11/4", "Made in USA, BC-4." $175-200. *Jerome Gundrum collection.*

Hires sign, tin, embossed, 9 3/8" x 27 7/8", marked "Made in USA, BN-3." Donaldson Art Sign Co., Covington, Kentucky. $55-75. *Jerome Gundrum collection.*

Hires signs, tin, embossed: Top: 4 7/8" x 13 3/4", marked "B-2." $50-75. Bottom: 9 3/4" x 27 5/8", marked "B-8." $75-100. *Jerome Gundrum collection.*

Hires display sign, cardboard, 16" x 28", "Black Cow" advertising. $15-25. *Jerome Gundrum collection.*

Mason's thermometer, tin, 16 1/16" x 5 7/8". The box this came in was stamped "salesman sample." $65-85. *Jerome Gundrum collection.*

Dad's sign, tin, 29 1/4" diameter, marked "PM-10. Printed in USA." $150-175. *Jerome Gundrum collection.*

Richardson sign, tin, double-sided, 9" x 12". Sign was top of a display rack. $25-35. *Jerome Gundrum collection.*

86

Hires signs, di-cut tin, c. 1950's. Large: 15 5/8" x 23 1/2", "Press sign Co., St Louis — BN-5." $85-105. Small: 8 1/16" x 11 7/8", marked "BN-4." $60-85. *Jerome Gundrum collection.*

Mason's sign, tin, embossed, self-framed, 13 15/16" x 17 11/16", "Stout Sign Co., St Louis, MO, M-158." $85-105. *Jerome Gundrum collection.*

Mason's sign, tin, 22" x 14". $85-105. *Jerome Gundrum collection.*

Frostie signs, thin molded plastic, 15 1/2" x 12 3/4". Adhesive strips on back for mounting on wall. The right one is also a thermometer. $15-25 each. *Jerome Gundrum collection.*

Triple XXX sign, cardboard, tin edge frame, 20 3/4" x 59 3/4". Bottom marked "Patented May 14, 1918; The Kemper-Thomas Co., Cincinnati, O." $85-115. *Jerome Gundrum collection.*

Ma's sign, tin, embossed, self-framed. Top blank portion is for store name. 34 1/8" x 57 3/4". $125-150. *Jerome Gundrum collection.*

Hires sign, molded plastic cover for an outdoor fluorescent light, 35 1/2" x 72". Marked "ELC/300 Made in USA." $85-115. *Jerome Gundrum collection.*

Dr. Swett's sign, tin, embossed, 31 7/8" x 55 7/8". $100-125. *Jerome Gundrum collection.*

Dr. Swett's
EARLY AMERICAN
ROOT BEER
RICH IN DEXTROSE

Dr. Swett's
EARLY AMERICAN
ROOT BEER
RICH IN DEXTROSE

Dr. Swett's signs, tin. Top: 9 1/4" x 27 3/16", marked "S-48-250." $35-50. Bottom: Self-framed, 17 7/8" x 54 1/8", marked "S-47-234." $65-85. *Jerome Gundrum collection.*

Hircs signs, tin, embossed, both marked "AAA Sign Co., Coitsville, Ohio." Both are enlarged replicas of the 1890's Hires trade cards. Signs are approximately 16 3/16" x 10". $8-12 each. *Jerome Gundrum collection.*

Dr. Swett's sign, cardboard, easel back, 18 1/8" x 13 3/4", marked "S-47-192 Litho in USA." $75-100. *Jerome Gundrum collection.*

Richardson lighted sign, plastic with wood base, marked "Pat. No. 2,361,354." 5 7/8" x 12 3/4" x 4 5/8". $45-65. *Jerome Gundrum collection.*

Mason's lighted sign, plastic and chrome, marked "Dualite Products, Inc., Cincinnati 27, O." 6 1/4" x 15 1/2". 3 3/4" deep. $40-60. *Jerome Gundrum collection.*

Buckeye lighted sign, glass and chrome, marked "Mfg by Ray-Flex Corp. Patent Nos. D-106116, D-111608." 13 1/4" x 16 3/4" x 5". $100-125. *Jerome Gundrum collection.*

Fanta sign, paper and foil, adhesive backing, 6" x 12". $10-15. *Jerome Gundrum collection.*

Hires sign, cardboard, 12 7/16" x 12". $65-85. *Jerome Gundrum collection.*

Dr. Swett's sign, cardboard, ll" x 21",
marked "Litho in USA, S-44-102" (it's
believed this may have been a display sign
in a street car). $60-85. *Jerome Gundrum
collection.*

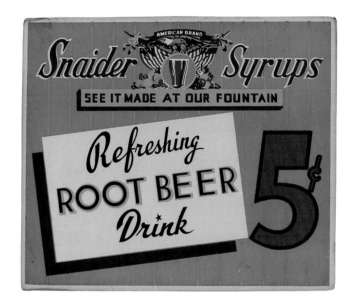

Snaider sign, cardboard, ll" x 13". $25-35.
Jerome Gundrum collection.

Linco sign, tin-framed cardboard (this type
of tin-framing design was copyrighted in
1918), 10 3/8" x 29 5/8". Marked at bottom
"Made in USA Pat. 1266194. The Kemper-
Thomas Co., Cin'ti, O." $85-105. *Jerome
Gundrum collection.*

Rochester sign, cardboard, 4" x 14". $20-30.
Jerome Gundrum collection.

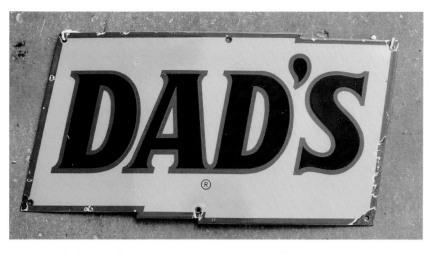

Dad's sign, di-cut, porcelain over tin, 9" x 17". $150-185. *Jerome Gundrum collection.*

Simpson Spring sign, tin, embossed. Lists their root beer (notice they also have nerve tonic!). $150-175. *Jerome Gundrum collection.*

Lakeside sign, thin, flexible tin. This sign is very old. $75-100. *Jerome Gundrum collection.*

R-LA sign, tin, embossed. $100-125. *Jerome Gundrum collection.*

Tower sign, tin, embossed, 19 1/4" x 8 1/2". $65-85. *Jerome Gundrum collection.*

Cott sign, wooden, bottle cap shape, 6 1/2"
diameter. $25-40. *Jerome Gundrum
collection.*

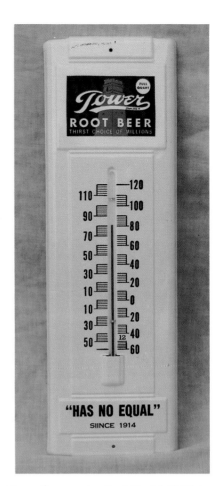

Tower thermometer, tin, 14" x 3 1/4" (Note:
the word "since" is misspelled as "siince").
$30-45. *Jerome Gundrum collection.*

Kreemo sign, cardboard, 10 5/8" x 6 15/16".
$25-30. *Jerome Gundrum collection.*

Wright thermometer, tin with glass tube, 5 3/
16" diameter. $25-30. *Jerome Gundrum
collection.*

Barq's sign, tin, embossed, 20 3/16" x 27 3/4". (Note: autographed by Mary Chapin Carpenter, the country/western singer who refers to "Barq's" in her song *I Feel Lucky*). $85-105. *Jerome Gundrum collection.*

Hires signs, tin, embossed. Left: 27 9/16" x 9 7/16", marked "B-27." Right: 27 7/16" x 9 7/8", marked "B-32." $125-150 each. *Jerome Gundrum collection.*

Hires sign, tin, embossed, "Printed in USA, BA-1", 9 1/2" x 27 3/8". $135-165. *Jerome Gundrum collection.*

Hires sign, tin, embossed, marked "BA-1", 9 1/2" x 27 3/4". $125-150. *Jerome Gundrum collection.*

Chapter 10
Miscellaneous

From small railroad cars, to fans, to extract bottles, to coolers, to paper dolls, the imaginative use of root beer objects in advertising is quite surprising. And remember, there is still much more out there waiting to be discovered. Good luck!

Dad's watches, manufactured by Quintel, purchased at Target Department stores in 1996. $15-25 each. *Dale Schatzberg collection.*

Togstad's extract, paper label, screw cap, 3 oz. $5-10. *John Reece collection.*

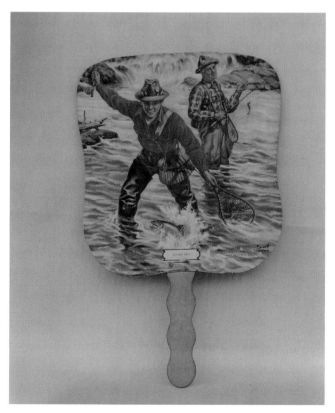

Frostie's hand fan, cardboard, "Second Best," 7 1/2" x 11 3/4", c. 1950s. $50-75.

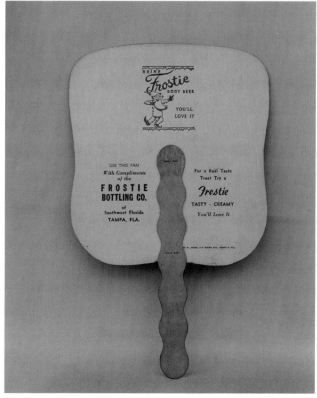

Frostie's hand fan, reverse side showing advertising.

Various crowns, cork-lined: Simpson Spring, Elwino and Mt. Olympus. $1-3 each.

Various crowns: L-R from top: Diamond, Corvallis, Qualtop, Michigan Maid, Sanders, Foust, Kastens, Aunt Mary's, Lollipop, Dodger, Celo, Bybee, Wilshire Club, Spurgeons, and Cricklers. $1-3 each.

"Tapper" root beer video game, approximately 6' high, 2 1/2' square. Date unknown. $300-400. *Courtesy of Reed Andrew.*

A&W candy box, root beer flavored jelly beans, c. 1996. Manufactured by Ferrara Pan Candy Co., Forest Park, Illinois. $1-2.

Print blocks. Left: Kist bottle, 2 1/16" x 11/16". Right: Hires, 2" x 3". Similar to rubber stamps, lettering is backward so when applied to a surface, the image comes out readable. $10-15 each. *Jerome Gundrum collection.*

Matchbooks: Old Dutch, Hires (box of stick matches), Powell's, Hydrox, and Mason's. $3-5 each. *Dale Schatzberg collection.*

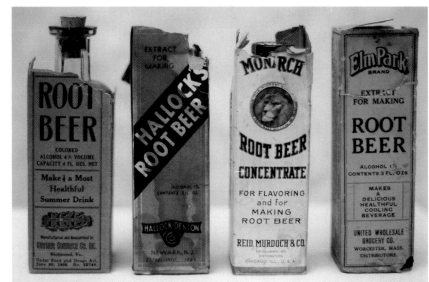

Various extracts. L-R: Interstate Commerce Co. (ICC), 4 oz., alcohol 4% volume, from Richmond, Virginia; Hallock's, 3 1/2 oz., alcohol 1%, from Newark, New Jersey; Monarch, from Chicago, Illinois; Elm Park, 3 oz., alcohol 1%, from Worcester, Massachusetts. $10-20 each. *Jerome Gundrum collection.*

Matchbooks: Wrights, Blue Rock, Duffy's. $1-3 each.

Matchbooks: Old Colony, Barq's, Barq's. $1-3 each.

Arctic drinking glass, 4" tall, 3" wide at mouth, 2" wide at base. Fluted design is on inside, smooth outside. Acid-etched lettering, c. 1910. $75-100. *Keith Austin collection.*

Ashtrays, ACL: Dog 'n Suds variations, $5-10 each; Hires, from the Hinner Bottling Co., Woodstock, Illinois. $20-25. *Dale Schatzberg collection.*

Hires full page newspaper ad from *The San Francisco Chronicle*, dated January 31, 1943. $20-25.

Dad's menu board, 24" x 13 1/2". $35-50. *Dale Schatzberg collection.*

A&W cooler, soft plastic, 12 1/2" high x 10 1/2" diameter. $20-30. *Jerome Gundrum collection.*

Frostie cooler, 14 5/8" x 12" x 14". $50-75. *Dale Schatzberg collection.*

Hires measuring glass, 8 oz., ACL, 4 3/4"
tall. $25-35. *Dale Schatzberg collection.*

Lyon's drinking glass, ACL, 5", syrup line.
$24-35. *Dale Schatzberg collection.*

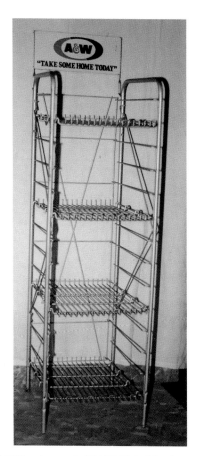

A&W rack, metal, 67 1/2" high. May have
been a display rack for gallon jugs. $75-100.
Dale Schatzberg collection.

A&W sign, canvas, 36" x 96". Notice the
rod pockets at each end for possible
hanging. $35-50. *Dale Schatzberg collec-
tion.*

Dog & Suds take home jug, plastic, 1
gallon. Has a spot where a slot can be cut to
become a bank. Also found in other colors.
$10-15. *Dale Schatzberg collection.*

Bardwell's punch bowl (for root beer, of course!), salt glaze, 11" high, 19 1/2" diameter at top. Has a patent number of 31737, dated Oct 31, 1899. $2500 (auction). *Courtesy of Pettigrew Auction House, Colorado Springs, Colorado.*

An inside look at the Bardwell's punch bowl. Center bowl is a permanent part of the large bowl, and is perforated around with half dollar size holes. This inner bowl's purpose may have been to hold the ice in one area while still being able to chill the drink. A small spout (not seen) near the bowl's bottom curve was possibly used to fill up a mug, as well as to drain the contents. Kind of a punch bowl dispenser - a very unique piece!

Hires pop machine, slider type, 42" high x 37" wide x 19 1/2" deep, 204 lbs. $400-600. *Dale Schatzberg collection.*

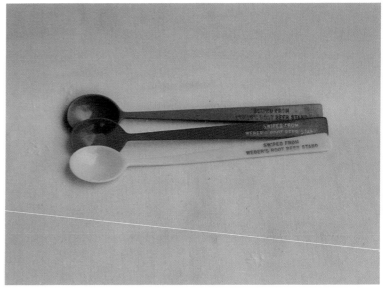

Weber's plastic spoons, 6" long. "Swiped from Weber's root beer stand" on handle. c. 1950s. $5-10 each.

Bokes ruler, tin. "Don't say root beer - say Bokes. In the frozen and frosted mug. Bokes is also the home of the famous Bokes twin burger - the most delicious treat in town." Two locations in Tucson, Arizona. $10-15.

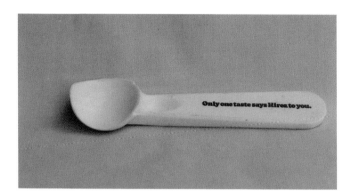

Hires ice cream scoop, 7" long, plastic (used for making delicious "Black cows" or root beer floats). $10-20.

Sno-Maid sewing pack, 3 1/2" x 6", folded cardboard holds about 70 gold eye needles. $10-20.

Hires record album, titled *Hires presents RCA Victor's Sound Spectaculars for 1959*, album number RCA SP33-15. Back side shows a malt shop scene advertising Hires. $10-15.

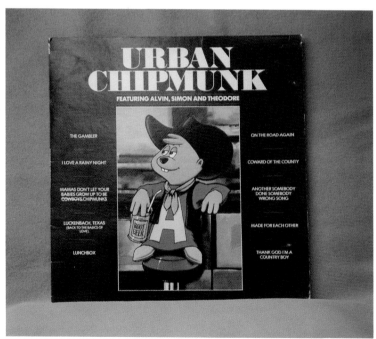

RCA record album, *Urban Chipmunk*, featuring Alvin the Chipmunk holding a can of generic root beer, c. 1981. $5-10.

Mug squeeze bottle for drinking water or root beer, plastic, 7 1/2", adjustable top hole. $3-5.

1919 keg hole plugger, plastic, 2 3/4" diameter. $1-3.

Barq's belt buckle, metal, 2" x 3 1/2". $15-20.

Barq's magazine ad, full page, 1950's juvenile delinquent movie theme, November 1992 issue of *Spy* magazine. $5-10.

Barrelhead belt buckle, metal, 3" x 2 1/2", c. 1976. "Old fashioned flavor - stands up to ice" engraved on back. $15-20.

Hires pocket mirror, metal frame, 1 7/8" diameter, c. 1890 (notice "cough" is spelled "couch"). $175-200.

Duffy's paper bag, 7 3/4" x 8 1/2" x 4 3/4" (could be a 6-pak carton in disguise!). $10-15.

Aunt Wick's root beer flavored powder mix. Place in glass, add water and ice. Presto - instant root beer! $1-2.

Ramblin' pin back, tin, 2" x 3". $5-10.

A&W spoon, plastic, 6 3/4" long. $3-5.

Durkee concentrate, 2 oz., plastic bottle, c. 1992. $1-3.

A&W valentine post card, 1 of 4 piece set, 4" x 6". Post card was free with purchase. $3-5.

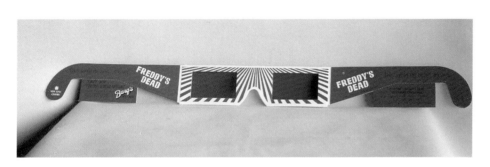

3-D glasses for the 1991 movie *Freddy's Dead, The Final Nightmare.* Features a special on Barq's root beer. 15 1/2" long. $5-10.

Frostie magnet, bottle shaped, 3" long. $1-3.

A&W stuffed bear, 4" tall (for decorative purposes only, not made as a toy). $3-5.

Duffy's post card, 3 1/2" x 5 1/2", dated 1942. Cards were locally mailed by Duffy's around the Denver, Colorado area to be redeemed for one free bottle of Duffy's root beer. $20-25.

Hires trade card, "And then the Fairies went to bed", 5" x 5 7/8", Hires advertising on reverse, c. 1895. $10-15.

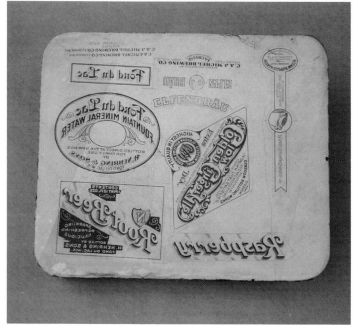

Stone lithograph for different labels from various breweries and beverage companies, including H. Nehring & Sons Root Beer from Fond Du Lac, Wisconsin, c. 1920s. Stone is 10" x 12" x 3" (about the size of a large phone book), and weighs 30 lbs. More labels are on the back side. Printing is backwards on the stone so when it is covered with ink and paper set to it, the printing will come out readable. $50-75.

1919 T-Shirt, cotton, (purchased in 1993 from the company). $5-10.

Frozen Hood's "Hoodsie Pops" wrappers, and Dad's ice cream bar wrapper. All 2 3/4" x 8 1/8". All recently found - and eaten!! $1-2 each. *Jerome Gundrum collection.*

Frostop redemption card, paper, 3 3/8" x 5 1/2". Reverse says "This ticket is good for one stein free Frostop root beer." $8-12. *Jerome Gundrum collection.*

Hires "Haskell-Coffin" tray, 10 1/2" x 13", by H.D. Beach Co., Coshocton, Ohio. $250 (auction, 1994). *Courtesy of Pettigrew Auction House, Colorado Springs, Colorado.*

Hires 5¢ tray, "Best Drink on Earth," 12" diameter. $1100 (auction, 1994). *Courtesy of Pettigrew Auction House, Colorado Springs, Colorado.*

Hires sign, reverse painting on glass, chain frame, 5" diameter. $1150 (auction, 1994). *Courtesy of Pettigrew Auction House, Colorado Springs, Colorado.*

Hires sign, reverse painting on glass, chain frame, 7" x 8", Mansfield & Co. makers. $2250 (auction, 1994). *Courtesy of Pettigrew Auction House, Colorado Springs, Colorado.*

Hires straw dispenser, lithographed, cast iron, 5" x 5" x 10". $3000 (auction, 1994). *Courtesy of Pettigrew Auction House, Colorado Springs, Colorado.*

Killer shake carton, 14 oz., c. 1990. The root beer is only one in a variety of flavors. $1-3.

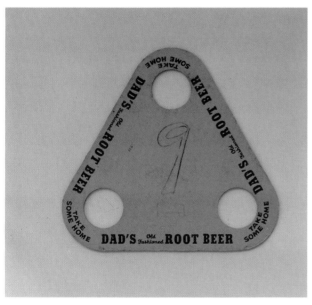

Dad's cardboard carrier/holder, 8 3/8" each side. Its exact function is a mystery. $10-15. *Dale Schatzberg collection.*

Solitaire extract, 3 oz., paper label, cork sealed. $5-10.

Richardson's display label, paper, 2" x 3 1/2". $1-2.

Ewald's drink spinner, lithographed metal, 2 3/4" x 1 3/8", Waterloo Bottling Co., Waterloo, Iowa. $100-150. *Dale Schatzberg collection.*

A&W jug, glass, 1/2 gallon, painted label, c. 1967. $25-30.

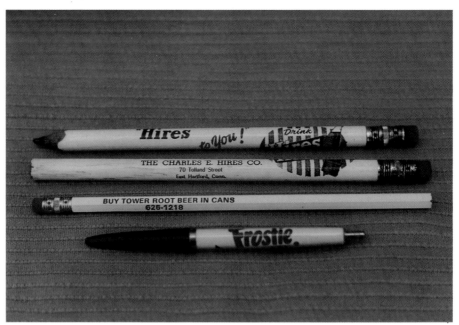

Pencils & pen: From top: Hires (top two the same); Tower; Frostie retractable ball point pen, 5" long. $3-5 each. *Jerome Gundrum collection.*

Stewart's mini mugs, with salt & pepper lids. $5-10 for set. *Dale Schatzberg collection.*

A&W bank, hard vinyl, approx 12-15" high. $40-50. *Dale Schatzberg collection.*

Berry's root beer pot, silver-plated pot metal. Bottom marked "Forbes Silverplate" (which was located in Meriden, Connecticut, and was in business from 1892 to 1896). It was not unheard of to serve hot root beer, and this would certainly have fulfilled that purpose! $200-250. *Jerome Gundrum collection.*

Hires miniature billboard, plastic with cardboard sign insert. 2 3/4" x 5". Matches the Hires H-O gauge train car. $5-10. *Dale Schatzberg collection.*

Hires train car, plastic, H-O gauge, 6" x 1 3/8" x 2". Silkscreen logos. Made by Tyco. $100-125.

Ma's bottle toppers, cardboard, dated 1944. $20-25 each. *Jerome Gundrum collection.*

Mason's bottle topper, cardboard, 5 1/2" x 8 1/2". $20-30.

Dad's bottle topper, cardboard, for 1/2 gallon "Papa" size, 8" x 12". $30-40.

Dad's bottle topper, cardboard, for 12 oz. "Junior" size. 7" x 9". $20-25.

Coated wax cone containers. Left: Hires, 1 qt. Right: Richardson's, 1 qt., has plastic clip-on for resealing. $15-25 each. *Dale Schatzberg collection.*

Mugs-Up coated wax cone, 1 qt., 9 3/4" high, Raytown, Missouri. $15-25. *Dale Schatzberg collection.*

Richardson's coated wax cone, 1 qt., 9 5/8" tall. $15-25.

A&W Lil' Brown Jug, plastic, 6 1/2" high (without plastic straw), 4" diameter, 1993. $1-3.

A&W root bear drink container, plastic, 9" tall (without plastic straw), 1994. Head twists off for refilling. $5-10.

Frostie clock, electric, plastic. 17" hand to hand, 18 1/2" high, c. 1980s. $25-40.

Frostie cuckoo clock, electric, main body is 10 1/2" x 16 1/2". Frostie man's face is where the cuckoo bird normally is. $75-100. *Dale Schatzberg collection.*

Frostie clock, plastic, electric, ll" x 22" x 3 3/4", tin back, made by Essex/NPI Company. $65-75.

Dad's clock, plastic, glass cover, electric, 15 3/4" square. $35-45. *Dale Schatzberg collection.*

Barq's clock, aluminum, 14" diameter. Grace Sign Co., St Louis, Missouri. $35-50. *Dale Schatzberg collection.*

Ma's clock, plastic, tin back, electric, neon lite, 16" x 16" x 3 1/2", General Indicator Corporation. $125-150.

Shade concentrate can, 6 fl oz., 3 13/16" tall. $5-10. *Jerome Gundrum collection.*

1919 tap knob, wooden with brass fittings, paper decal two-sided, 3 5/8" x 5 3/4". $10-15.

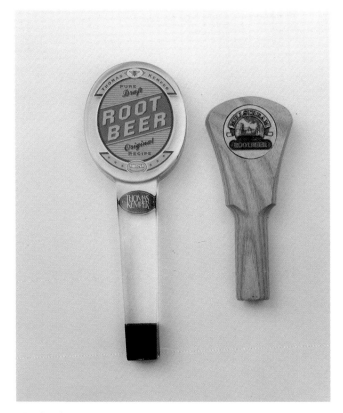

Tap handles: Thomas Kemper, clear acrylic with colored emblem embedded, 9" x 3 1/4" x 7/8"; Mill Stream, oakwood with laser engraved marble insert, 6" x 2 1/2" x 1". $10-15 each. *Dale Schatzberg collection.*

Thomas Kemper tap knob, wooden with brass fittings, paper decal two-sided, 2 5/8" x 7 1/4". $10-15.

Variety of tap handles, plastic, 2-3" high. $3-5 each. *Dale Schatzberg collection.*

Dad's tap knob, plastic, 3" x 1 1/2". $5-10.

Bethesda wooden case. $50-75. *Jerome Gundrum collection.*

Howel's wooden case, l0" x 12" x 18 1/2". $50-60.

Thomas Kemper tap knob, solid wood, bottle-shaped, paper label, 7 1/2" high, screw-in hole in bottom. $20-25.

Belfast wooden case, 8" x 13" x l9 1/2". $40-50.

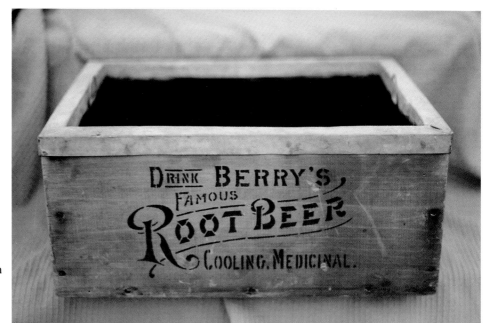

Berry's wooden case, inside is zinc-lined (possibly to hold ice for cooling some type of liquid refreshment bottle containers). There are clips on each end of the case. Evidence suggests these may be for attaching a neck strap to aid in carrying the case by seller/vendors at special events such as baseball games. $100-135. *Jerome Gundrum collection.*

Brownie wooden case, steel-banded corners, cardboard dividers inside, l0 1/2" x ll 1/2" x 17 1/2". $50-75. *Dale Schatzberg collection.*

Wooden cases: Tom Sawyer, 12 1/2" x 17" x 12 1/2". Dr. Swett's, 10 1/4" x 17 3/4" x 11 3/4". $35-50 each. *Jerome Gundrum collection.*

A&W pinback, tin, 2 1/4" diameter. $5-10.

Mug pinback, tin, 3" diameter. $5-10.

A&W pinback, Dennis the Menace Vari-Vue, 3" diameter, changes pictures by tilting, by Pictorial Products Inc., Mt. Vernon, New York. Patent # 2,815,310. $15-20. *Dale Schatzberg collection.*

This is the second picture seen when the Dennis the Menace Vari-Vue is tilted.

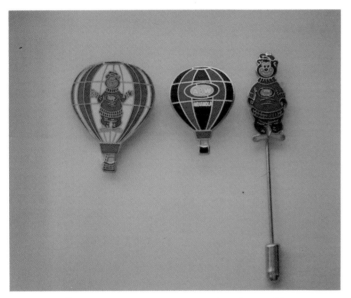

A&W collar pins and tie tack. These may have been sold as souvenirs for the Indianola, Iowa balloon races, held over a ten to fifteen year period. $10-15 each. *Dale Schatzberg collection.*

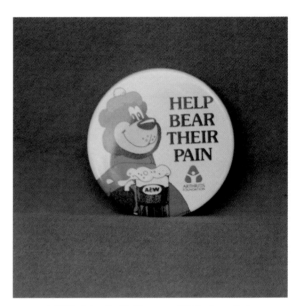

A&W pinback, 3" diameter, "Help bear their pain - Arthritis Foundation". $5-10.

Various pinbacks, 3-3 1/2" diameter. Clockwise, from left: IBC, Dads, Mug, A&W root bear, Dads. $5-10 each.

A&W can, inflatable, 49" high, 23" diameter, c. 1990. $35-50.

A&W "Great Root Bear Float" raft, inflatable, plastic, 32" x 52". $35-50. *Dale Schatzberg collection.*

A&W pumpkin, inflatable, 36" x 36", c. 1992. $25-30.

Reverse side of the A&W inflatable pumpkin.

Dr. Swett's pocket mirror, tin and celluloid, 3" diameter. $125-150. *Jerome Gundrum collection.*

Dad's bottle opener, brass, 4 1/4" x 1 5/8".
$5-10.

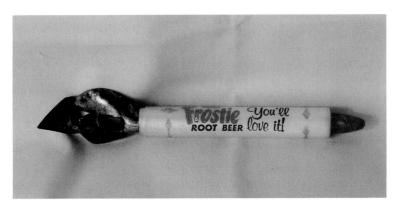

Frostie bottle opener/can piercer, plastic handle, 6". This type was developed by Mr. Lipic of St. Louis, Missouri in the early 1950s. $15-20.

Hires bait cooler, pressed cardboard, l0" x 12 1/2", marked "Magic Minnow Bucket," Jardier Inc., Milwaukee, Wisconsin. $50-75. *Dale Schatzberg collection.*

Hires cooler, aluminum, 28" x 13" x 13 1/2". Cronstrom Manufacturing Co., Minneapolis, Minnesota. $50-75. *Dale Schatzberg collection.*

Bottle openers. Top: Glueck's, key-shaped, patented 1901. Says "key to Glueck's root beer. Glix Beverages." Has Prest-O-Lite key (the square hole was used as a wrench to open a valve on carbide tanks located on early automobile running boards. These tanks provided gas for the headlights). $25-35. Bottom: Barq's wall mount. $10-15. *Dale Schatzberg collection.*

Barrelhead cooler, tin, lithographed, 13 1/2" high x 11 1/2" diameter. Rope handle. $25-35. *Dale Schatzberg collection.*

Dad's cooler, can shaped, styrofoam lined, 14" high, 8 1/4" diameter, by Ehco, Inc. Holds a 6-can pak and a couple of sandwiches! $15-20.

A&W miniature truck. "75th Anniversary." $50-75. *Dave & Kathy Nader collection.*

A&W miniature truck. $50-75. *Dave & Kathy Nader collection.*

Metal car replicas: A&W bank made by Ertle Co., 1/25 scale; Dad's (not a bank) made by 1st Gear Inc., 1/34 scale. C. 1990s. $25-35 each. *Dale Schatzberg collection.*

Metal car replica banks: Hires and Barq's made by the Ertle Co., 1/25 scale. C. 1990s. $25-35 each. *Dale Schatzberg collection.*

A&W miniature truck. $50-75. *Dave & Kathy Nader collection.*

Barq's miniature truck. $50-75. *Dave & Kathy Nader collection.*

A&W miniature car. $50-75. *Dave & Kathy Nader collection.*

Barq's miniature truck. $50-75. *Dave & Kathy Nader collection.*

Winter Garden patch, cloth, 7" x ll". San Antonio, Texas. $15-25. *Hank Reidling collection.*

Triple XXX ticket for a free treat at the broadway "Thirst Station" in Galveston, Texas. $5-10. *Hank Reidling collection.*

Wright's drinking glass, ACL, no syrup line, 4". $25-35. *Hank Reidling collection.*

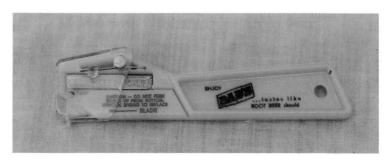

Dad's razor knife, plastic and metal, adjustable, 5 3/8" long, Patent # 2730800. $1-3. *Jerome Gundrum collection.*

Elwood's train car, "G" scale (about the size of a loaf of bread!). Manufactured by Model Die Casting Inc., #G4655. $50-75. *Dave & Kathy Nader collection.*

Dad's train car, "G" scale (about the size of a loaf of bread!). Manufactured by Bachmann Industries Inc., Philadelphia, Pennsylvania. $50-75. *Dave & Kathy Nader collection.*

Dad's frozen confections: ice cream on left; ice cream bars on right. $1-2 each. *Jerome Gundrum collection.*

Mugs-Up token, cardboard, 1 1/4" diameter. Reverse says "Save 15. Jiffy Gallon Club. 1 gallon free with 15." $2-5. *Hank Reidling collection.*

A&W wooden token for one free root beer. 1 1/2" diameter. Reverse says "Larry's A&W drive-in, Larned, Kansas." $2-5. *Hank Reidling collection.*

Baumeister sticker, paper, 6" x 11 3/4". $3-5. *Jerome Gundrum collection.*

Hires magazine ad, 11 1/4" x 16 1/2", back page of *The Ladies Home Journal*, June 1895 issue. $15-20. *Jerome Gundrum collection.*

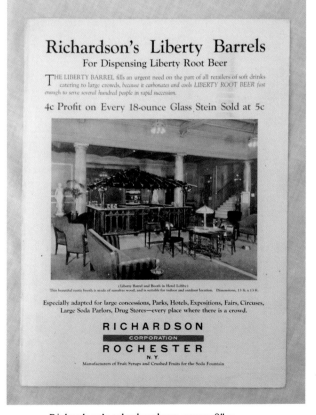

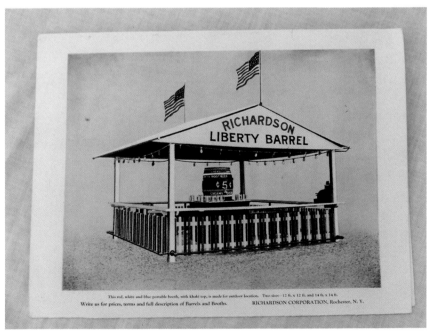

Richardson's sales brochure, paper, 9" x 12". Part of a six page brochure advertising different soda fountain barrels. $10-15. *Jerome Gundrum collection.*

Richardson's sales brochure, paper, 9" x 12". Another part of the six page brochure advertising different soda fountain barrel features. $10-15. *Jerome Gundrum collection.*

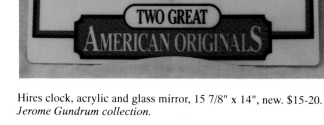

Hires dispenser plate, molded aluminum, 6 1/8" x 8". (a similar plate with "1876" in the center is pictured in my first book). $25-35. *Jerome Gundrum collection.*

Hires clock, acrylic and glass mirror, 15 7/8" x 14", new. $15-20. *Jerome Gundrum collection.*

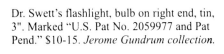

A&W magnet, plastic material over magnet, 2 3/8" diameter. $1-3. *Jerome Gundrum collection.*

Dr. Swett's flashlight, bulb on right end, tin, 3". Marked "U.S. Pat No. 2059977 and Pat Pend." $10-15. *Jerome Gundrum collection.*

- **GREAT TASTE!**
- **CAFFEINE FREE!**
- **COMBINE WITH ICE CREAM FOR A DELICIOUS ROOT BEER FLOAT!**
- **TERRIFIC RESALE ITEM FOR RESTAURANTS AND CONVENIENCE STORES!**
- **NOW WITH TWIST OFF CAP!**

I.B.C. magnets: Top: bottle cap shaped, plastic, 2 3/8" diameter. Bottom: rubber, 3" x 9". $1-3 each. *Jerome Gundrum collection.*

Hires menu board, tin, embossed, 28 7/8" x 15 3/8", "Made in USA, BB-3." $75-95. *Jerome Gundrum collection.*

Hires door push, tin, 4" x 23 3/4" (sign portion), "No. 4143 Printed in USA. Stout Sign Co., St. Louis, MO." $65-85. *Jerome Gundrum collection.*

Dr. Swett's tip tray, tin, 4 1/4" diameter. $100-125. *Jerome Gundrum collection.*

Mason's chalkboard, tin, embossed, 29 1/2" x 19 1/2", marked "Donasco, 68-168." $65-85. *Jerome Gundrum collection.*

Mug "Hager the Horrible" hat, cloth, dated 1991. $3-8. *Modeled by Andrew Gundrum.*

Sweet Sixteen T-Shirt, cloth. $8-12. *Modeled by Amy Gundrum.*

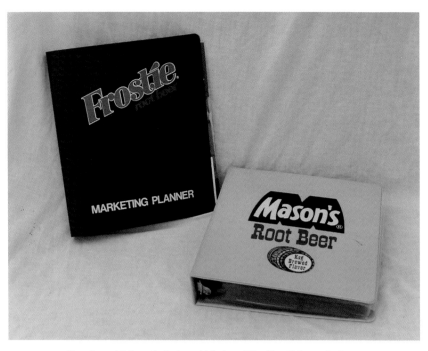

Frostie and Mason's 3-ringed binders. The Frostie's marketing planner is from 1982. $10-15 each. *Jerome Gundrum collection.*

Hires belt buckle, cast metal, 2 3/4" diameter. $10-15. *Jerome Gundrum collection.*

Hires door push, tin, 3 1/2" x 11 1/2", "Made in USA - BL-1." $55-65. *Jerome Gundrum collection.*

A&W deck of cards. $10-15. *Jerome Gundrum collection.*

Dybala's Spring beverage list, including their root beer. Cardboard, 19 15/16" x 9 1/4". "Nelke(N) Hornell, NY." $15-25. *Jerome Gundrum collection.*

Taylor's extract, 3 oz., paper label, from Trenton, New Jersey. $5-10. *Jerome Gundrum collection.*

Dr. Swett's bottle carrier, 6-pak, cardboard, 1940's, 12" x 8" x 5". $15-20. *Jerome Gundrum collection.*

Florida extract bottle, embossed, 3 oz. $10-15. *Jerome Gundrum collection.*

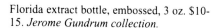

Indian extract, 3 oz., from Boston, Massachusetts. Not known in any way to be related to "Baker's Indian," although the picture logos are similar. $10-15. *Jerome Gundrum collection.*

Three Star extract, 3 oz., from New York, New York. $10-15. *Jerome Gundrum collection.*

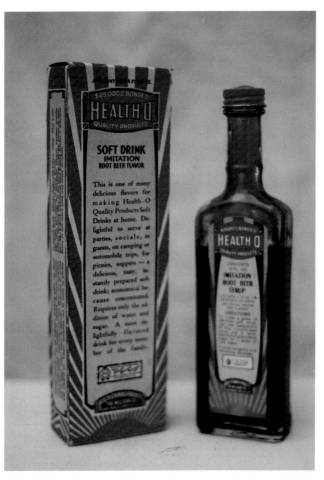

Health-O extract (syrup), 4 oz., box is 8 5/18" high, from Cincinnati, Ohio. $5-10. *Jerome Gundrum collection.*

Extracts, 3 oz. each: Gloria, from Springfield, Massachusetts; Lecroy's, from Camden, New Jersey; Highland, from Boston, Massachusetts. $10-15 each. *Jerome Gundrum collection.*

French's extract, 3 oz., from Rochester, New York and Philadelphia, Pennsylvania. $5-10. *Jerome Gundrum collection.*

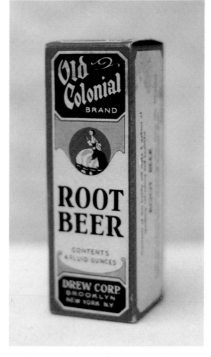

Old Colonial extract, 4 oz., from Brooklyn, New York. $5-10. *Jerome Gundrum collection.*

Thompson & Taylor (T&T) extract, 3 oz., from Chicago, Illinois. $5-10. *Jerome Gundrum collection.*

Royal Worcester extract, 3 oz., from Worcester, Massachusetts. $5-10. *Jerome Gundrum collection.*

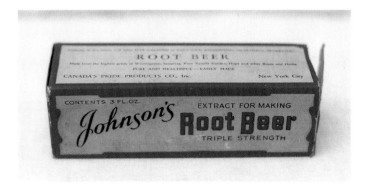

Johnson's extract, 3 oz., from New York, New York. $5-10. *Jerome Gundrum collection.*

Dove extract, 3 oz., from Cincinnati, Ohio. $5-10. *Jerome Gundrum collection.*

Ma's sign, tin, 2 1/8" x 26 1/2". This is part of a door push or a carton display rack. $25-30. *Jerome Gundrum collection.*

Zanol extract, 3 oz., from Cincinnati, Ohio. $5-10. *Jerome Gundrum collection.*

Old Kentucky extract, 3 oz., from Boston, Massachusetts. $5-10. *Jerome Gundrum collection.*

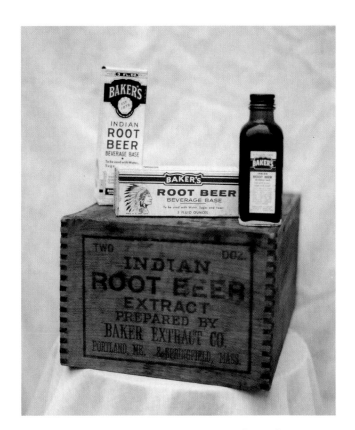

Baker's "Indian" extract items. Bottles are 3 oz., box is wooden with dovetail corners, 5 1/2" x 10 3/4" x 9 9/16". Bottles, $5-10 each; box, $15-20. *Jerome Gundrum collection.*

Menu chalkboards, tin: Top: **Dad's, 27 7/8" x 19 15/16", Press Sign Co., St Louis, 3-73.** Center: Dad's, same size, Press Sign Co., St Louis, 7-76, also "PM-68." Bottom: Frostie, 23 1/4" x 17 1/2". $50-65 each. *Jerome Gundrum collection.*

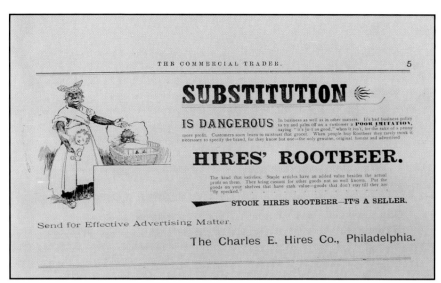

Hires ad, "Substitution" in *The Commercial Trader*, New Haven, Connecticut, dated May 20, 1899. $10-15. *Jerome Gundrum collection.*

Hires bottle display stand, tin, 5 1/4" tall, 4 1/4" diameter. Sign marked "BS-1." $95-115. *Jerome Gundrum collection.*

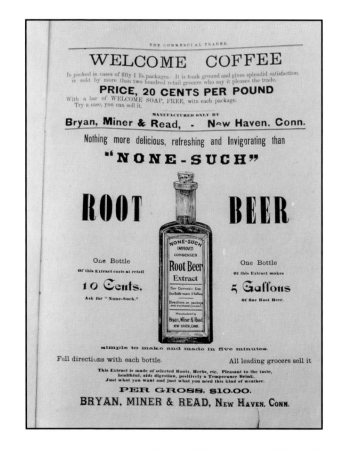

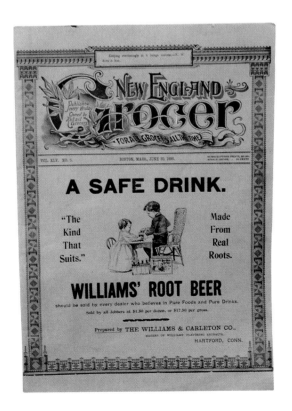

"None-Such" extract ad, 3/4 page of *The Commercial Trader*, New Haven, Connecticut, dated May 20, 1899. $10-15. *Jerome Gundrum collection.*

William's full, front page ad from the *New England Grocer*, Boston, Massachusetts, dated June 30, 1899. 15" x 10 1/2". $10-15. *Jerome Gundrum collection.*

William's full, front page ad from the *New England Grocer*, Boston, Massachusetts, dated June 23, 1899. 15" x 10 1/2". $10-15. *Jerome Gundrum collection.*

Hires front page ad, "Third & Last Call", 15" x 10 1/2", from the *New England Grocer*, Boston, Massachusetts, dated May 26, 1899. $10-15. *Jerome Gundrum collection.*

Close-up of glass plate (this one is for Barq's) used by Armstrong for making bottle caps. 72 crowns per glass plate, measures 14" x 17". $10-15. *Jerome Gundrum collection.*

Old Kentucky pitcher, ceramic/pottery, 8 1/16" tall, bottom marked "Hand painted in Japan" (same style and design as the mug, which is pictured in my first book). $25-35. *Jerome Gundrum collection.*

132

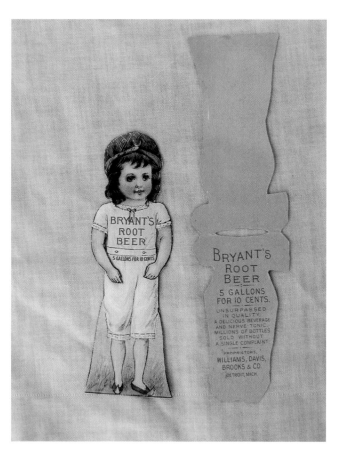

Bryant's cut-out paper dolls, approx 4 5/8" x 2". Outfits slip over the dolls' heads (see separate picture). Top, L-R: Little Bo Peep, Cinderella, Little Red Riding Hood. Bottom, L-R: Jack the Giant Killer, Little Boy Blue, Aladdin. $10-15 each. *Jerome Gundrum collection.*

A closer look at the Bryant's cut-out paper dolls. This is Aladdin with outside clothes removed, showing extract advertisement. Each paper doll has same advertisement.

Allen's trade cards, paper. Sizes, L-R: 4 13/16" x 3 3/16"; 4 1/2" x 2 3/4"; 4 1/2" x 2 3/4" (Note: The left card was the one enlarged and duplicated to make the new, tin sign featured on page 56 in the chapter on signs). $10-20 each. *Jerome Gundrum collection.*

Hires Christmas bottle hanger, heavy paper, approx 3 1/2" x 8". By moving the wreath slighly, Santa's eyes look upward and "Hi-Ya" appears in his mouth. $25-35. *Jerome Gundrum collection.*

Knapp's trade card, 3" x 5", two-sided. Act I is on the front; Act 2 on the reverse. A two-act stage play! $10-15. *Jerome Gundrum collection.*

Act 2 (reverse side), of the Knapp's trade card.

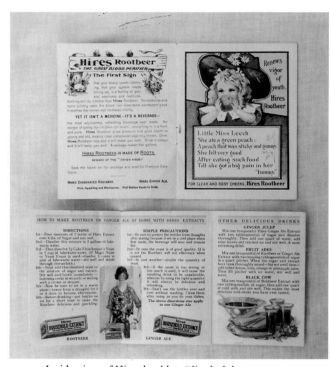

Hires booklets. Left: "Jingle Jokes for Little Folks", 4 13/16" x 3 3/4", dated 1901. $25-35. Right: "Hires Extracts for Root Beer at Home", 4 1/8" x 3" (see separate picture for inside view). $10-15. *Jerome Gundrum collection.*

Inside view of Hires booklets "Jingle Jokes for Little Folks" and "Hires Extracts for Root Beer at Home."

Hires booklets: Left: "Distinctive Quality", date unknown. Center: "Hires Magic Story", dated 1934, 4" x 6", 6 pages, each page has a rubbing or scratch area to reveal a picture. Right: "Hires 1939 Football Book" of schedules and information (see separate picture on next page for inside view). $20-30 each. *Jerome Gundrum collection.*

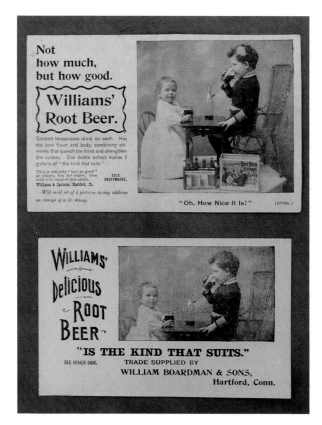

Inside view of Hires booklets "Distinctive Quality" and "Hires Magic Story." The football book is not shown.

William's trade cards, paper, c. 1890's. Yes, they are black and white, and are separate cards (although they appear to be the reverse of each other). The top is 3 11/16" x 6" (notice that the extract box is the same one that appears on page 140 in full color). The bottom is 3 5/16" x 5 9/16". $10-15 each. *Jerome Gundrum collection.*

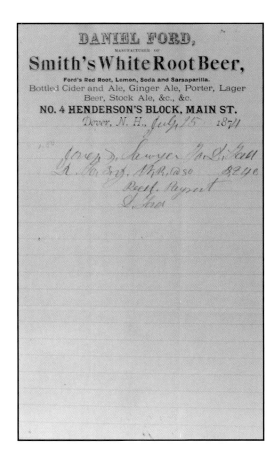

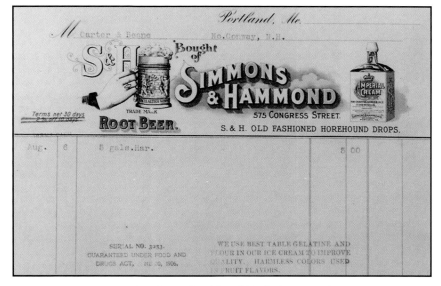

S&H (Simmons & Hammond) letterhead for a bill of sale, paper, 5 1/4" x 8". (note: Food & Drug Act stamp of 1906 is at the bottom). $5-10. *Jerome Gundrum collection.*

Smith's letterhead for a bill of sale, 5 1/4" x 8", dated July 25, 1874. (Note: this is two years before Charles Hires introduced his root beer at the Philadelphia Centennial Exposition in 1876! See this book's introduction for more information about the significance of these dates). $5-10. *Jerome Gundrum collection.*

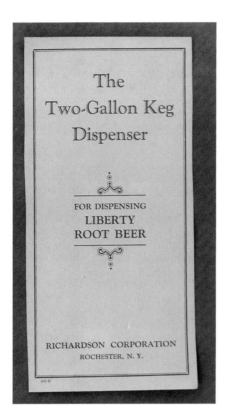

Liberty advertising flyer, two-sided paper, 6 7/16" x 3 1/8". (see separate picture for reverse side). $10-15. *Jerome Gundrum collection.*

Reverse side of two-sided Liberty advertising flyer.

Patches, embroidered cloth: Hires, 3 1/2" x 3 1/8"; Barq's, 2 1/16" x 3 5/16";.Ted's, 2 1/16" x 3 5/16." $5-10 each. *Jerome Gundrum collection.*

Miscellaneous items: Richie, cardboard, reverse says "Richie says a cooking stove on Pike's Peak. Drink Richardson root beer;" Barq's cardboard token, 1" diameter; Frostie metal token, reverse says "Good for one bottle....;" Dad's pencil clip, tin; Hires tie-tack or lapel pin, says "110 years genuine Hires root beer since 1876." $3-6 each. *Jerome Gundrum collection.*

Ted's wooden case, 10 1/4" x 18" x 12". Holds two dozen 12 oz. bottles. $15-20. *Jerome Gundrum collection.*

Hires door push, tin, metal brackets, c. 1950's, 5 1/8" x 17 7/8". Reverse says "Thank you - please call again". Press Sign Co., St. Louis, BP-14. $65-90. *Jerome Gundrum collection.*

Hires paper cups, wax coated, 4 3/16" high, c. 1950's. $1-3 each. *Jerome Gundrum collection.*

Snyder's paper cups, wax coated, 4 9/16" high. $1-3 each. *Jerome Gundrum collection.*

Mason's bottle carrier, for outdoor events. Embossed, aluminum outside, 3 3/4" x 17 1/2" x 11 7/16". "Property of Mason's Bottling Co., Jamestown, NY." $20-30. *Jerome Gundrum collection.*

Hires "free gift" ball, sponge rubber, 2 3/16" diameter. Hung around bottle neck and was free with purchase of Hires product (ball only was pictured in my first book). $15-25. *Jerome Gundrum collection.*

Mason's door push, metal, 2 1/2" x 32 7/8". $65-85. *Jerome Gundrum collection.*

Dad's "free gift" of salt & pepper shakers, plastic. Shakers measure 1 9/16" x 1" x 1/2". No marking on shakers, but package hung around bottle neck and was free with purchase. $10-15. *Jerome Gundrum collection.*

Hires extract box, wooden, 5 1/2" x 7 1/4" x 5 3/4", dovetail corners. $15-25. *Jerome Gundrum collection.*

Hires "soda jerk" hat, paper, 3 1/8" x 10 3/4", c. 1950's. Marked "Made and printed in USA by Servis Cap., P.O. Box 2512, Phila 47, Pennsylvania." $10-15. *Jerome Gundrum collection.*

Hires bottle topper, cardboard, 6 1/8" x 3 1/2", "Litho in USA, BQ-1." $35-45. *Jerome Gundrum collection.*

Hires banner, cloth with brass grommets, 36 1/2" x 56 1/2", marked "Code BK-L, Litho in USA." $65-95. *Displayed by Andrew & Amy Gundrum.*

Mason's bottle display, cardboard, 10" x 11 1/2", "Litho in USA, P-303." $30-50. *Jerome Gundrum collection.*

Barq's door push, tin, 3 1/16" x 19 1/2". $25-35. *Jerome Gundrum collection.*

Dad's coin bank, wood with metal bands, coin slot in top, 6 1/4" high. $20-25. *Jerome Gundrum collection.*

Hires basketball and backboard, rubber/plastic/metal. Backboard measures 18 1/2" x 24". $30-45. *Jerome Gundrum collection.*

Dad's and A&W's plastic mugs, 6 5/8" high. $1-3 each. *Jerome Gundrum collection.*

Hires paper decal on glass, 2 7/8" x 14". $5-10. *Jerome Gundrum collection.*

William's extract shipping boxes, wood with paper labels. Large box: 15" x 22 1/4" x 17 1/8". Holds one gross of extracts. $65-85. Small box: 7 5/16" x 9 3/4" x 5 1/8". Holds one dozen extracts. See separate close-up picture. $45-65. *Jerome Gundrum collection.*

Close-up of William's paper label from the small, one dozen extract wooden box.

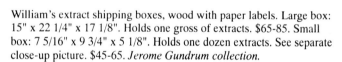

Lambert's extract box, wooden with paper labels, 5 1/4" x 24" x 12". $35-50. *Jerome Gundrum collection.*

Frostie thermometer, 12" diameter, glass front. $35-50. *Dale Schatzberg collection.*

Ted's thermometer, plastic front, 12" diameter, recently manufactured. $20-30. *Jerome Gundrum collection.*

Bardwell's "canteen" jug, pottery, 10 7/8" x 10" x 4 3/4". Made by White's Pottery in Utica, New York. This is the original one; the reproduction, with further information, is available in my first book. $250-300. *Jerome Gundrum collection.*

Twang thermometer, glass and tin, 12 1/4" diameter. $125-150. *Jerome Gundrum collection.*

Mason's thermometer, glass and tin, 12 1/4"
diameter. Marked on bottom "68-117."
$100-125. *Jerome Gundrum collection.*

Mammoth extract box, wooden, dovetail
corners, paper labels, wire hinges, 7 1/2" x
13 1/2" x 9 1/4", from Hartford, Connecticut. $35-55. *Jerome Gundrum collection.*

Woosies pencil, metal and wood. Pencil can be turned around and
inserted back into shaft, becoming hidden. The other end is a bottle
opener. Says "root beer" on other side. $10-15. *Jerome Gundrum
collection.*

Williams full display for one dozen extracts, 2 3/4 oz. bottles, cork
sealed. Directions for making root beer are in six different languages
on each box. From East Hartford, Connecticut. $95-115. *Jerome
Gundrum collection.*

A&W napkin holder, tin and metal, 7 3/8" x
4 3/8" x 5 3/4". $25-45. *Jerome Gundrum
collection.*

Grandma's cookie jar, ceramic, pull-tab soda can shaped, 9" tall (to flat lid), 6 1/2" diameter. See separate picture for sugar cookie recipe on reverse of jar. $50-75. *Jerome Gundrum collection.*

Reverse side of Grandma's cookie jar, with sugar cookie recipe.

"Root Beer Master." Has no brand name, and its function and purpose are somewhat of a mystery. It is made of heavy metal, covered with porcelain. The valves and pressure gauge may have something to do with "pressurized carbonation!" $125-150. *Jerome Gundrum collection.*

Top: Frostie can piercer/bottle opener (commonly referred to as the "church key" type), c. 1940's. Bottom: Ma's bottle opener, wire-formed type, patented in 1915. $10-15 each. *Jerome Gundrum collection.*

Krueger bottle stopper, metal with rubber washer, marked "by Seal Again Bottle Stopper Co., New York; Patent no. 2157937" (same company as the Krueger Beer Company). $15-20. *Jerome Gundrum collection.*

Hires pen knife, 3" long, celluloid handle, key chain loop. $5-10. *Jerome Gundrum collection.*

Hires watch fob, brass, 1 5/8" x 1 1/2", leather strap. Picture of Hires boy standing and pointing, with mug in right hand. $100-125. *Jerome Gundrum collection.*

Click 1974 calendar, cardboard face with tin frame. $20-25. *Jerome Gundrum collection.*

Richardson calendar pad holder, tin, 4" x 5 3/4". $15-20. *Jerome Gundrum collection.*

Click menu board, tin, slate writing surface. $50-75. *Jerome Gundrum collection.*

Frosties belt buckle, cast metal, 2 1/2" x 3 3/4". Says "Frostie root beer racing team, McLaren racing car, driven by A1 Loquasto" (Loquasto drove this car at an Indy 500 race during the mid-1960s). $15-20. *Jerome Gundrum collection.*

Rob's bottle carrier, heavy cardboard, paper label, holds 24 bottles, 7 3/4" x 17 5/16" x 11 3/8", dated 2-61, from Charles C. Copeland Co., Inc., Milton & Brockton, Massachusetts. $20-25. *Jerome Gundrum collection.*

Generic syrup bottle, label under glass, 12" tall. $75-100. *Jerome Gundrum collection.*

Mason's 10 oz. bottle carrier, cardboard. $10-15. *Jerome Gundrum collection.*

Churchill "Aloha" fountain glass with syrup line, 5 9/16" tall. $50-75. *Jerome Gundrum collection.*

Hires 12 oz. bottle carrier, cardboard. $10-15. *Jerome Gundrum collection.*

Dr. Swett's 10 oz. bottle carrier, cardboard. $10-15. *Jerome Gundrum collection.*

Buckeye back bar bottle, pottery, 7 1/16" high. Metal, jigger-style top, is missing. $150-200. *Jerome Gundrum collection.*

Ma's 12 oz. bottle carrier, cardboard. $10-15. *Jerome Gundrum collection.*

Leary's 12 oz. bottle carrier, cardboard. $10-15. *Jerome Gundrum collection.*

Goody bottle topper, cardboard, 5 1/2" x 7". $10-15. *Jerome Gundrum collection.*

Virginia Dare bottle topper, cardboard, 5" x 5 3/4". $25-30. *Jerome Gundrum collection.*

Goody bottle topper, cardboard, 5 1/2" x 7". $10-15. *Jerome Gundrum collection.*

Kreemo bottle topper, cardboard, 6 1/2" x 8". $10-15. *Jerome Gundrum collection.*

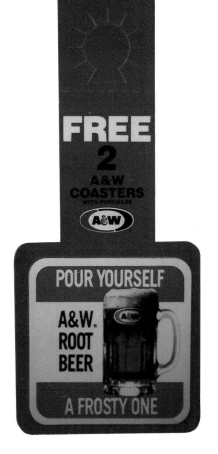

Aunt Wick's packs of flavored powder for mixing one glass or one quart of root beer. $1-2. *Jerome Gundrum collection.*

A&W bottle hanger with two "free gift" coasters attached, cardboard. Coasters are 3 1/2" square. $10-15. *Jerome Gundrum collection.*

Edy's "Root Beer Float" ice cream, 1/2 gallon wax/cardboard container, "Limited Edition." $1-2. *Jerome Gundrum collection.*

Kool-Aid pack of root beer flavored powder, c. 1950s. $5-10. *Jerome Gundrum collection.*

Root beer flavored tea by East India Tea & Coffee Ltd, San Francisco, California. $1-2. *Jerome Gundrum collection.*

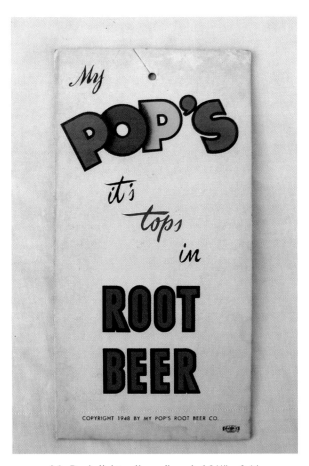

My Pop's light pull, cardboard, 6 3/4" x 3 1/2", 1948. $15-20. *Jerome Gundrum collection.*

Hires radio/lamp combo, 17" high (Note: this is a fake! A Hires label has been pasted on the shade, and part of a label was pasted to the base. Beware!! The dealer who had this was claiming it was genuine and had it priced at $475). $5-10. *Jerome Gundrum collection.*

Richardson bottle carrier, cardboard, World's Fair Selection from 1939. $15-25. *Jerome Gundrum collection.*

Cover of the 1974 record album *Streetlife Serenade*, by Billy Joel. Features the song *Root Beer Rag*. $3-5. *Jerome Gundrum collection.*

Nufizz instant pop, a root beer flavored mixture. Cardboard/foil, 8" x 9", 1958. Has the "Good Housekeeping Seal." $15-20. *Jerome Gundrum collection.*

Mason's cigarette lighter, can shaped, tin, 5" high. $15-20. *Jerome Gundrum collection.*

Kreemo carrier for 6 bottles, tin, paper label, 9 1/2" x 8" x 5 1/2". The same carrier has been seen with the identical Kreemo label lithographed on the front. It is impossible to determine which (if either) may be a fake. $20-25. *Jerome Gundrum collection.*

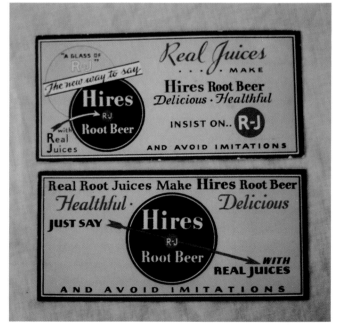

Hires ink blotters, cardboard, 3" x 6". $10-15 each. *Jerome Gundrum collection.*

Richardson decal for its wooden barrel dispensers, 6" x 7 7/8". $10-15. *Jerome Gundrum collection.*

Vaughan's salt & pepper shakers, glass with pewter lids, 5 3/4" high. Both front and back sides shown. $15-20. *Jerome Gundrum collection.*

Various Dad's pin-backs, celluloid. The Dad's "Black Cow" measures 4" in diameter. $5-10 each. *Jerome Gundrum collection.*

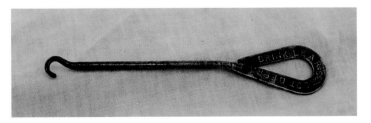

Lear's button hook, pressed metal, 5 1/2" long. Says "Drink Lears root beer," c. 1920s. $35-50. *Jerome Gundrum collection.*

Hires pin-back, celluloid, 2" diameter. $3-6. *Jerome Gundrum collection.*

A&W golf towel, terrycloth, 17" x 24". $5-10. *Jerome Gundrum collection.*

Hires paper weights. Plastic, quart bottle shaped, 5 3/16" tall. $10-15 each. *Jerome Gundrum collection.*

Generic root beer pitcher, pottery with pewter lid, about 12" tall, beautifully designed! $750-850. *Jerome Gundrum collection.*

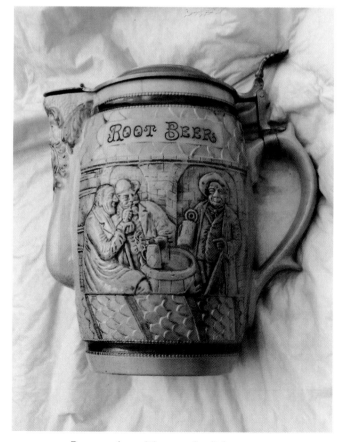

Reverse view of the generic pitcher.

Index of Brand Names

In my first book, 831 root beer brands were substantiated. Here, 338 additional brands, not previously listed in my first book, are identified by an asterisk (*). Of those brands already mentioned in my first book, some are also indexed here to provide updated information or to reference new pictures within this book.